Haunted
Connecticut

Haunted Connecticut

Ghosts and Strange Phenomena of the Constitution State

Cheri Revai

Illustrations by Heather Adel Wiggins

STACKPOLE
BOOKS

Published by
STACKPOLE BOOKS
5067 Ritter Road
Mechanicsburg, PA 17055
www.stackpolebooks.com

Printed in the United States of America

10 9 8 7 6 5 4 3 2 1

FIRST EDITION

Design by Beth Oberholtzer
Cover design by Caroline Stover

Illustrations by Heather Adele Wiggins

Library of Congress Cataloging-in-Publication Data

Ravai, Cheri, 1963–

    Haunted Connecticut : ghosts and strange phenomena of the Constitution State / by Cheri Revai. –1st ed.
       p.   cm.
    Includes bibliographical references.
    ISBN-13: 978-0-8117-3296-3 (pbk.)
    ISBN-10: 0-8117-3296-7 (pbk)
    1. Haunted places–Connecticut. 2. Ghosts–Connecticut. 3. Parapsychology. I. Title.
BF1472.U6R474 2006
133.109746–dc22
                                         2006009390

To Leland

Contents

Introduction

I CHOSE CONNECTICUT WHEN MY PUBLISHER ASKED ME WHICH STATE I'D like to write the next *Haunted* book about. It didn't take me long to decide it would have to be the Constitution State. After all, I've only ever lived in two states, and Connecticut was one of them, even if I was too young to remember it. We lived two houses down from the haunted Nathan Hale Homestead in Coventry, which Mom describes as a beautiful, picturesque area—a small bedroom community in 1963, with big pine trees surrounding the houses. She said it was the kind of place that gives you a warm, fuzzy feeling to go home to. I'm not sure she'd have said that if we'd lived two houses down! When I found out Connecticut was one of my choices, I had a sudden urge to reconnect with this place of my past that my parents describe so fondly. So I chose Connecticut, and am I ever glad I did.

Connecticut was first settled by English Puritans from Massachusetts in 1633. By 1639, it had devised a democratic form of government called the Fundamental Orders, which were actually the basis for the United States Constitution, hence its nickname, the Constitution State. The second-smallest state in New England, Connecticut is flanked by New York State on the west, Rhode Island to the east, and Long Island Sound on the south. The Connecticut River virtually divides the state in half. The northwestern region has forested hills and mountains, but two-thirds of the state consist of open, relatively flat land. The state, which has nine counties, can be broken down into five regions: Northwestern Connecticut, or the Litchfield Hills; Southwestern Connecticut, or Fairfield County,

also known as the Gold Coast; Central Connecticut, or the River Valley; South Central Connecticut, or the Greater New Haven region; and Eastern Connecticut, or Mystic Country, which includes Connecticut's "Quiet Corner" in its northeastern section. Every region, large or small, has its stories to tell, so I've broken the fifty-one tales in this book into five sections by region.

Qui Transtulit Sustinet, or "He who transplanted still sustains," is an apt state motto for Connecticut, because it is a state of immigrants who settled there long ago. A similar motto would be apt for a book about ghosts: *"He who came still remains."* That certainly seems to be the case, for many haunted places exist throughout Connecticut where former residents appear to have remained long after they passed away. It certainly seems that way in Dudleytown and the famous "Village of Ghostly Voices" in Pomfret. Connecticut has so many famous ghosts, in fact, that I can't list them all here, but some that I've included in this book are Elisabeth, or the Green Lady of Burlington; Hanna Cranna, the witch-turned-ghost of Monroe; the Stratford poltergeists at Phelps Mansion; Union Cemetery's White Lady of Easton; Abigail, a ghost with good reason to haunt Pettibone Tavern; Midnight Mary, who lingers near her tombstone, which warns people to stay away at midnight; and the ghosts of the Old State House, Benton Homestead, Old Union Trust Building, Nathan Hale Homestead, Lighthouse Inn, and Ledge Light Lighthouse.

Connecticut is also known for haunted islands; phantom ships, trains, and planes; sightings of UFOs, aliens, and Men in Black; and encounters with Bigfoot and an evil black dog. There have been plenty of strange atmospheric anomalies, such as Connecticut's Dark Day; solid clouds that came crashing down from the sky in the Litchfield Hills in 1758; the Moodus Noises, which have yet to be fully understood; and Notch Hollow near Bolton, where car windows fog over for no apparent reason while passing an abandoned railroad track.

Connecticut, like the rest of seventeenth-century New England, had its witch hunts, but mercifully, the state did not endure as much bloodshed as Salem suffered. Connecticut has seen heroes, such as Nathan Hale, Abraham Davenport, and the jurors in the Stamford witch trials, as well as eccentrics: the Leatherman, who walked a 365-mile loop wearing sixty pounds of leather for twenty-six years nonstop, except to sleep in caves or under the stars each night;

Sarah Pardee Winchester, who moved from Connecticut to California, where she designed the "most mysterious house ever built"; and two men who allegedly followed instructions from God and the Devil, respectively. One was told to build Holy Land USA, a miniature village of famous biblical scenes depicting the life of Jesus, which is now abandoned; the other was told by little demons to build a village of tiny houses just right for their size, the Little People's Village. If all of that is not enough, you can read about the Jewett City vampires and the amazing D. D. Home, said to be the greatest medium ever to walk the earth.

I'll say this for Connecticut: It's more diversified than I ever imagined. As Governor M. Jodi Rell says on CTvisit.com: "Connecticut is all about . . . fun! In just about every form you can imagine." Indeed, the stories in this book, covering the whole spectrum of the paranormal, are fun to read . . . in a satisfyingly spooky sort of way.

Northwestern Connecticut

NORTHWESTERN CONNECTICUT IS SYNONYMOUS WITH THE LITCHFIELD Hills region. This area has the quintessential New England scenery, with rocky peaks, waterfalls, fertile valleys and farmland, covered bridges, forested hills, plains, vineyards, and small towns. Couple its geographic features with the man-made creations, like the countless museums, antique shops, craft centers, and Connecticut's biggest water park, and you can see why the region attracts the rich and famous from nearby New York City to what is often considered the "Hamptons of Connecticut." The forty-nine towns making up this region have also attracted a number of interesting folks over the years, in the form of eccentrics, entrepreneurs, and egotistical fanatics—and we have them to thank for their legacy of lurid legends, many of which you'll read about in greater detail in the pages that follow.

The Dudleytown Curse of Cornwall brought misfortune to the lives of its residents, including a onetime editor of the *New York Post* and a famous cancer doctor from New York City. Waterbury's Holy Land USA once drew thousands of believers to the site, which is now in ruins. The miniature biblical world was the brainchild of evangelist John Greco, who claimed to be following God's direct orders to construct the theme park. By contrast, also lying in ruins is the Little People's Village of Middlebury, which was built for the little devils who "spoke" to an unstable husband and wife who then followed their orders. There was also the famous Leatherman, who walked an endless 365-mile circle between the Connecticut and Hudson Rivers, sleeping at exactly the same locations outdoors every thirty-four days for twenty-six years straight. And of course, there are ghosts. Carousel Gardens by Candlelite Restaurant in Seymour and the Green Lady and Guntown Cemeteries all have well-publicized ghost stories to share. Throw in a few Bigfoot sightings and one of the largest UFO flaps in history, and you will begin to realize what a melting pot of paranormal paradoxes rural New England boasts.

Carousel Gardens by Candlelite

The historic Victorian mansion at 153 North Street in Seymour was built in 1894 by William Henry Harrison Wooster. Many people, including the owners of the mansion, believe that Wooster and his two children are still floating around somewhere on the grounds of the mansion, which is now a popular restaurant called Carousel Gardens by Candlelite. Lights flicker, photographs taken in the mansion often reveal orbs, objects mysteriously tumble off shelves or actually levitate before incredulous eyes, music that is playing changes in midsong from dinner music to heavy metal, and on and on. But the Sciaraffa family, who has owned and operated Carousel Gardens since 1993, find the paranormal disturbances, which are becoming less frequent, more fun than spooky.

According to the restaurant's website, www.carouselgardens.com, the ghostly antics add spice to their American cuisine. An employee once saw and heard a cat upstairs that has never been found. The distinct sound of a glass falling on the floor of the bar and shattering was once heard by a group of people nearby, yet no actual glass—broken or otherwise—was ever found. Another time, a glass of water flew across a table and smashed as seven guests watched in disbelief. The glass had been at the only empty spot at the table, so the guests invited Ruth, the alleged ghost, to join them. Ruth was the original owner's daughter, to whom employees and guests usually attribute the ghostly antics. The feisty phantom was also blamed for sending spoons and ladles hurtling off a ceiling rack onto the head of a chef who was being rude to a waitress who had popped into the kitchen to ask him a question. You go, girl!

Deborah Sciaraffa said they have no reason to want the ghosts to leave. Carousel Gardens is visited by paranormal investigators, television talk-show crews, and people just looking for some great food and a chance encounter with Ruth, the ladle-throwing ghost.

Dudleytown Curse

Death, dementia, disappearances—Dudleytown. The small, deserted hamlet of Cornwall is located about a thousand feet above the village of Dudleytown. You might feel somewhat disoriented and insignificant beneath the towering trees of the dense forest, where darkness reigns more often than light in the shadows of three surrounding mountains. The terrain is rock-laden and difficult to traverse, much less cultivate or inhabit. The land is hostile, and not just geologically speaking. At least that's what the legends would have you believe. If that's not a good enough reason to stay away, perhaps the $75 minimum fine for trespassing or parking on the property is enough incentive to heed the landowner's warnings. The Dark Entry Forest Association (DEF) has every right to try to preserve the area deemed "forever wild" on the organization's original charter in 1924—they bought it for the peace and tranquility they hoped it would afford them. But Dudleytown is dubbed one of America's most haunted places and has become legendary for its famous "Dudleytown Curse," drawing the curious to the mysterious settlement like moths to an open flame—that is, until recently, when the Connecticut State Police started strictly enforcing the no-trespassing rule because of escalating vandalism at the site. Police will now seek out and destroy—er, I mean *prosecute*—shameless trespassers. So, you've been warned. For the time being, merely reading about the strange happenings at Dudleytown will have to suffice.

It all started with the beheading of one Edmund Dudley, who plotted to overthrow King Henry VIII in England in 1510. But merely decapitating one man apparently wasn't enough punishment for the treason, so his entire lineage was cursed (though no source seems to say by whom) to the effect that all Dudley family descendants from that point on would be surrounded by horror and death. And so began four hundred years of bad luck for the Dudleys, including those who settled in Dudleytown beginning in 1748. There is some controversy as to whether the three brothers for whom Dudleytown was named—Gideon, Barzillai, and Abiel—were even from the original Edmund Dudley lineage, but there is no question as to the misfortune that befell them once they settled there. Curse or not, something bizarre and destructive began to affect the residents of Dudleytown who were in any way associated with the Dudley brothers.

It began with a mysterious epidemic that killed the entire Adoniram Carter family in 1774. Their relatives, the Nathaniel Carter family, were so saddened by the tragedy that they packed up and moved to Binghamton, New York. But shortly after their move, Nathaniel and his wife and infant child were killed by Indians, who then took the remaining three children as captives to Canada, where two of them were ransomed; the third, a son, married an Indian girl. In 1804, another Dudleytown resident, Sarah Fye, was struck by lightning on her front porch and killed instantly. Her husband, General Herman Swift, was said to have gone insane at the news of his wife's unexpected passing.

Mary Cheney was born in Dudleytown and married Horace Greeley, the founder of the *New York Tribune*, who was most famous for his phrase "Go West, young man." In 1872, she committed suicide a week before her husband lost his bid for presidency. Then in the late 1800s, John Patrick Brophy's family was struck by the curse. Mrs. Brophy died of consumption, and shortly afterward, their two children vanished in the woods, never to be found. The Brophy home burned to the ground, though some believe Brophy may have set the fire himself. Regardless, Brophy left Dudleytown and was never seen again.

Dudleytown sat vacant for about twenty years, when Dr. William Clark, a cancer specialist from New York City, came upon the site in 1920. He fell in love with its serenity and seclusion and purchased the tract of land along with several friends and colleagues, who formed the Dark Entry Forest Association. In the mid-1920s, Dr. Clark was away on an emergency call in New York City and returned several days later to find that his wife had gone completely insane, allegedly following an attack of something terrifying that came out of the forest. She had to be institutionalized for the rest of her life.

Since that incident, no other such tragedies have been reported by anyone living near Dudleytown; however, many individuals had what they believed were paranormal experiences while visiting the site, when it was still permitted. Unexplainable anomalies have appeared in many photographs, the eerie sound of complete silence occasionally gets disturbed by incoherent voices that seem to start from afar and work their way closer, and strange shapes have taken form before people's eyes, including black moving masses that seemed to follow individuals and a wolflike shadow that two people saw watching them from the woods. One lady said she had seen it five times over the course of twenty-five years. That same woman lost her brakes fleeing the site the last time she visited it recently. Turned out the caliper was snapped completely off. No wonder Dudleytown is often considered the most haunted place in New England. And no wonder people are warned not to go there. They may be disturbing more than just the peace.

Fairfield County UFO Flap

During the 1980s, the Hudson Valley was the site of a number of high-profile flaps over UFOs that were witnessed by thousands of people. The wave of sightings became known as the Hudson Valley Boomerang Sightings, and the entire region quickly attained UFO hot-spot status. While much of the ado focused on New York's Pine Bush area, Fairfield County, Connecticut, was not to be outdone. Mark Packo thoroughly investigated and documented the sightings for the Mutual UFO Network (MUFON) of Connecticut. His investigations of two very active dates in 1985 and 1989 provided detailed accounts of the typical boomerang sightings by most who were fortunate enough to witness the phenomenon.

According to Packo, on March 21, 1985, reports of huge UFOs were phoned in to authorities from New Fairfield, Bethel, Danbury, Trumbull, Bridgeport, Milford, Orange, Derby, Ansonia, Naugatuck, and Middlefield. Most accounts of the sighting in Fairfield County are fairly similar, describing a large round or oval saucer outlined by red and white lights, a "flattened football," a large blimp, or an object with red and white lights on its underside. It was said to be slower than a plane, very large (like a football field), and either silent or making a low humming noise. The UFO was not at all shy of populated areas, often hovering or moving slowly over the major highways (I-95 and I-84), Housatonic Parkway, and shopping centers.

Because of the sheer volume of witnesses over such a widespread area, many newspapers reported on the sightings in the days following the light show, including the *Danbury News-Times, Bethel Homes News, Bridgeport Post, Milford Citizen, Ansonia Evening Sentinel, Middletown Press,* and *Waterbury Republic.*

The August 31, 1989, sightings differed from the 1985 sightings in that the object in question was more often boomerang-shaped, although this one also had red and either white or yellow lights around its circumference. The cities of Stratford, Trumbull, Shelton, and Bridgeport played host to this UFO, and as with the 1985 sightings, scores of eyewitnesses described the object surprisingly similarly. Again, the object was unconcerned with high visibility. All witnesses to the aerial anomaly in the skies of Northwestern Connecticut that night agreed that the object was very large and angular, with both flashing and steady lights. It was described as V-shaped, L-shaped, or triangular; similar to the hull of a submarine; and as "a floating triangle of lights." It moved very slowly and at a low altitude, hovering just above treetops or quiet side streets for a moment, before moving on unhurriedly.

Both of these UFOs were sighted by thousands of witnesses, many of whom were policemen, scientists, and researchers. Though the shape differed from one UFO to the other four years later, in both cases everyone agreed that the objects were extremely large, quiet, and slow moving—and something unidentifiable that they had never seen before.

Green Lady Cemetery

Every region has its haunted cemeteries, and two of Northwestern Connecticut's most active ones are the Seventh Day Baptist Cemetery, or Green Lady Cemetery, in Burlington and Gunntown Cemetery in Naugatuck. The Green Lady Cemetery is located on a dirt road called Upson Street in the Litchfield Hills of Burlington and is so named for its ghost, Elisabeth, who drowned in a nearby swamp after her husband was unable, for whatever reason, to save her. She is believed to have taken the form of a female apparition surrounded in a green mist that drifts down the dirt road and hangs about her grave, which one source said is the only grave left that hasn't been affected by vandals. A couple taking photographs of the fall foliage were astonished to find a yellowish green haze in front of Elisabeth's grave in one photograph, while no other photographs from the entire shoot revealed similar anomalies. They had felt a strange presence around them while they were taking the photograph. In the same cemetery, mysterious lights are often seen on the road, looking like a flashlight or lantern carried by an unseen person or headlights unattached to any actual car. Maybe Elisabeth's husband is still searching for her in the swamp from another dimension, unaware that she drowned.

Guntown Cemetery in Naugatuck doesn't need a nickname to make it memorable. Even world-famous paranormal researchers Ed and Lorraine Warren have declared it officially haunted. The most frequently reported phenomenon there is the sound of children's laughter and music that begins in the surrounding woods, then closes in on the listener until it seems to be inside the cemetery. An inordinate number of stray, solid black dogs have been spotted near the cemetery, even though it is in a remote, unpopulated area. Many people, especially those familiar with Connecticut's Black Dog of Meriden, believe this is a foreboding sign of death. Sometimes a person clearly sees the black dog in the cemetery but his or her companions see nothing. Many photographs taken at Guntown Cemetery depict spirit energy in the form of orbs, globules, and mists, and orbs of every color can be seen flitting about the grounds with the naked eye.

Holy Land USA

On a hilltop overlooking I-84 in Waterbury is a lighted cross with three unlit crosses to its right, the one in the center bearing a likeness of Jesus with his right arm missing. Though the Golgotha scene has become by default a place marker for the city of Waterbury, it originated as a high-visibility advertisement for Holy Land USA, a miniature biblical land on Slocum Road designed by an eccentric evangelist in 1956. Today the area lies mostly in ruins, giving it an air of creepiness even if it's not haunted—but some swear it is.

Lawyer and evangelist John Baptist Greco solicited the help of local volunteers who called themselves the Catholic Campaigners for Christ of Connecticut to construct a miniature biblical village depicting various scenes from Jesus' life and death. Greco claimed that his orders to build such a place came directly from God. Believers flocked here by the thousands during its glory days, but when Greco passed away in 1986, thirty years after Holy Land opened, the nuns to whom he had left it were unable to maintain its care and operation. Eventually it was closed and fell into ruin. The old, white buildings that once made up a mini-Jerusalem and the decapitated and dismembered statues of the Wise Men's camels that remain today must make trespassers feel uneasy. Nevertheless, only one solitary ghost sighting has been reported. In 1985, a year before Greco died, a stunned witness watched a female apparition get into a phantom car near the front gate and drive off, vanishing into thin air before his very eyes. The incident made the local paper the next day. It would have been even more remarkable had they seen a phantom camel carry off a phantom Wise Man into the night, but we'll take what we can get!

The Leatherman

The Leatherman is thought to actually have been one Jules Bourglay, born in Lyons, France, in the 1820s. He came from a lower-middle-class family but fell in love with the daughter of a wealthy leather merchant. His only hope of receiving permission to marry her was to prove himself in her father's family business. It wasn't long before Bourglay had earned enough trust, through hard work and loyalty, to be given the important task of purchasing leather in the open market. One fateful day in 1855, however, he made a very large leather purchase at what he believed to be a ridiculously good price. Sadly, he hadn't been keeping up with the news regarding the latest technology in leather manufacturing. The reason such a large amount of leather was being sold so cheaply was because the price of leather was about to drop dramatically as a result of a breakthrough in leather tanning. The large purchase of leather Bourglay had made could be sold only at a substantial loss—and that spelled financial ruin for his intended's family business. Now Bourglay would never receive permission to marry the woman he loved.

Too ashamed to return to his own family, Bourglay wandered around Lyons until a physician agreed to take him in. That arrangement worked for two years, but then Bourglay disappeared and was

never seen in France again. In 1862, a man fitting Bourglay's description showed up in Harwinton, Connecticut—the leather may have given him away. Here he began his famous trek—a sort of self-penance, if you will. Bourglay became an itinerant eccentric with a strange compulsion to walk endlessly in a 365-mile circle between the Connecticut and Hudson Rivers, never straying from his original route. He seemed not to know English, for he spoke only in grunts and communicated with gestures, and he was dressed in leather from head to toe in a getup estimated to weigh sixty pounds. But it was well worth its weight in leather for the protection it afforded him against years of unforgiving New England winters. You see, the Leatherman, as he became known, slept only under the stars and in caves along his route. Though he met many kind folks along his way who offered him food and lodging, he respectfully declined. He walked more than ten miles a day for more than twenty-six years straight, stopping at the same caves precisely every thirty-four days and, in fact, preparing each cave with firewood for his next stop there before moving on to the next one. Some of the towns he passed through were Harwinton, Bristol, Forestville, Southington, Kensington, Berlin, Middletown, Danbury, New Milford, Roxbury, Woodbury, Watertown, and Plymouth.

The first and only time he was slowed by the weather was in the Blizzard of 1888. In his midsixties by then, he fell ill and was thrown off his schedule by four days. He eventually died in a cave in Briar Cliff Manor, New York, never fully recovering his strength from that illness. His spirit is believed to still linger as it passes through the caves where the Leatherman stopped over and over during life, as he makes his way eternally along the familiar route. Some are easier to get to than others, and the one called Leatherman Cave is probably the most popular. On the Mattatuck Trail in Watertown, it is best reached by starting at Black Rock State Park in Thomaston and following the well-marked trail for about two miles into the woods. As you climb the steep and rocky trail leading to the cave, imagine how the Leatherman must have felt repeating those same steps so many times with at least sixty pounds on his back for thirty years—about 360 times! If that's not supernatural, I don't know what is.

Lillinonah's Leap

Charles M. Skinner wrote of Lillinonah's Leap in *Myths and Legends of Our Own Times: As to Buried Treasure* . . . :

> At New Milford, Connecticut, they'll show you Falls Mountain, with the cairn erected by his tribe in 1735 to Chief Waramaug, who wished to be buried there, so that, when he was cold and lonely in the other life, he could return to his body and muse on the lovely landscape that he so enjoyed. The will-o'-the-wisp flickered on the mountain's edge at night, and flecks of dew-vapor that floated from the wood by day were sometimes thought to be the spirit of the Chief. He had a daughter, Lillinonah, whose story is related to Lover's Leap, on the riverward side of the mountain.

Chief Waramaug and the Pootatuck tribe lived high on a hilltop overlooking the Housatonic River near New Milford in the early 1700s. The chief was admired not only for his good taste in the impressive long house he had constructed for his tribe, but also, especially, for his good and kind nature, as far as Indian chiefs go. His daughter Lillinonah was his pride and joy. At eighteen years of age, she had become a beauty and shared her father's traits of compassion. Many young Indian braves hoped to win her father's approval and Lillinonah's hand in marriage.

But one cold, wintry day, Lillinonah was out walking in the woods when she came upon a young white man who was having obvious difficulty walking. He seemed disoriented and ill, and her heart went out to him. She went to him at once, allowing him to lean on her for support as they made their way back to her village, where he could recover. Her father and the rest of the tribe refused to help Lillinonah nurse the man to health, so she did it herself, and by the end of the winter, he was fully recovered. Much to her father's dismay, the two had fallen deeply in love and asked for his blessings in their union. Her father was furious and said that with all of the Indian suitors she could choose from, he would never allow her to marry outside of the tribe—a white man, no less. The words hurt Lillinonah to her very core, and she refused to eat or take care of herself. Finally, after months of watching his once beautiful daughter waste away, Chief Waramaug agreed that they could be married.

After all that, you'd think the two young lovers wouldn't have wasted a moment before the ceremony, but for some reason lost to history, the couple agreed that the man would return to his white settlement for one final winter and make his people aware of his plans of marrying an Indian woman. He would return in the spring, and they would marry in the summer. The separation was very hard on the tender Lillinonah, so as spring drew near, her mood improved in anticipation of her lover's return. But return he did not. Spring turned to summer, and summer turned to fall.

Sensing Lillinonah's despondency, the Chief arranged a marriage for her, thinking it would give her something to live for, but when she got wind of his plans, she couldn't bear the thought of marrying another. So she went to the Housatonic riverbank, climbed into a canoe, and was quickly carried off in the turbulent water toward the dangerous falls. Just as she approached the edge of the falls, in a narrow gap of the river now known as Lover's Leap or Lillinonah's Leap, she threw her paddles overboard and sat back in the canoe to await her fate. At the moment she did that, she saw her long-lost lover standing helplessly on a cliff overlooking the falls. He had returned after all! But it was too late. He leaped into the water just as she stood in her boat and cried out to him, and the two joined together in an embrace as they plunged over the falls to their death. When their bodies were found, they were wrapped around each other. Although it went against Indian custom of the time, Chief Waramaug buried the lovers side by side on top of a hill overlooking the spot where they met their fate. When the chief died many years later, he too was buried at Lillinonah's Leap, beside his beloved daughter and would-be son-in-law.

When Connecticut Light and Power built the Shepaug Dam in 1955 as a source of flood control and harnessing hydroelectricity from the mighty Housatonic River, three lakes set aside by calmer waters were inadvertently created. The largest and northernmost of these was named Lake Lillinonah, after the Indian maiden who found true love, lost it, and then reclaimed it at the moment of her death. The lake is a popular haven for water recreation, wildlife, and fishing.

Litchfield County Bigfoot Sightings

The Bigfoot sightings in Litchfield County are unremarkable to the researcher in that they boast the usual characteristics: large, unexplainable footprints; big, hairy, stinky creatures spotted in remote areas; and eerie screams and screeches. But this is the first time I've heard of a horse being scared to death by Bigfoot.

According to the Gulf Coast Bigfoot Research Organization (GCBRO), in the fall of 1997, a man and his horse had stopped at a stream for a drink when the man noticed a large footprint twice the size of his own in the streambed. Then he smelled the telltale odor of a Bigfoot creature, and that was enough to make him ride off quickly on his horse—with a real, live Bigfoot in hot pursuit. Bigfoot took off after the fleeing man and horse with such a ruckus that the earth seemed to shake and branches were heard cracking in its wake. The creature easily caught up with the man but thankfully was separated from them by a stone wall. Still, it kept an eerie pace with the pair until it was sure they were well on their way away from the area, and then it slowed down and finally stopped, but not without a few cursory screams as if to say, "And don't come back again!" No need to worry, though, for the man wouldn't have returned if his life depended on it, and his horse never recovered from the traumatic experience and died shortly thereafter.

Little People's Village

"Come out, come out wherever you are . . ." The abandoned Little People's Village in Middlebury looks as if it could have been a wonderland for playful tots at one time, but it wasn't, I assure you. The legends have it as something much more sinister, and if you walk down the lonely dirt road toward the mysterious deserted settlement when the air is still and the night is silent, you might be inclined to agree (but don't try this, as the property is private). The negative energy left behind by not-so-dearly departed entities is palpable.

The village in the woods once consisted of many little stone houses with authentic and usable tiny architectural elements inside, such as miniature staircases. The houses, which stood merely three or four feet tall, were said to have been constructed for little demon people. There are several variations to the legend of the Little People, but most agree that a husband built the diminutive neighborhood for the beings his wife believed coexisted with them. She believed she was Queen of the Little People and, as such, required an appropriate throne, which her husband dutifully built into the side of the hill. It's one of the only remaining structures on the site today, along with the couple's own house, which has barred windows, probably to keep the little devils out.

In some versions of the legend, the wife (aka Queen) was instructed to kill her husband after he dared to sit on her throne, but then the little demons killed the wife—or persuaded her to do the deed herself. In other versions, the hapless husband couldn't stand any more of his wife's mental instability and bizarre requests, so he killed her and then himself. Whatever actually happened, the throne is said to have become jinxed, so that anyone who sits on it will die in seven days, or seven years, or in a short period of time, depending on who's telling the story.

No physical evidence, beyond the remnants of the little houses, has ever been found for an actual civilization of little people in that location, demonic or otherwise, and I have not been able to uncover any history on the couple that allegedly built the little settlement and lived there. But though their creations were little, their legend is larger than life.

Solid Clouds

Some colonialists called it fog; others said it was clouds. But whatever it was that descended on Northwestern Connecticut early one morning in 1758 landed with such force that it shattered into pieces and caused damage to property. One firsthand account, according to an online article by Robert L. Sheridan, said, "It came down from the heavens in great bodies, and knocked down the walls of our houses." Under the heading "Crazy Clouds and Fog," on a paranormal phenomena blog called *When Nature Goes Nuts*, is described "a fog of 'strange and extraordinary appearance'" that "arrived in thick bodies that would 'break' when it struck buildings." Though it broke like ice, the colonists insisted that the so-called fog "emitted such heat that they found it difficult to breathe near it!"

The 1758 volume of *The Annual Register of World Events* reported the same phenomenon, saying:

> . . . about sunrise, at this place was a fog of so strange and extraordinary appearance, that it filled us all with amazement. It came in great bodies, like thick clouds, down to earth, and in its way, striking against the houses, would break and fall down the sides in great bodies, rolling over and over. It resembled the thick steam rising from boiling wort, and was attended with such heat that we could hardly breathe.

Nobody has ever explained this bizarre weather anomaly.

Southwestern Connecticut

SOUTHWESTERN CONNECTICUT CONSISTS OF JUST FIFTEEN TOWNS OR cities in Fairfield County, including Bridgeport, the state's largest city, and Stamford, which places fourth in population. This region is also called "the Gold Coast," because the rich and famous from nearby New York City make their homes here.

Although it's the smallest of Connecticut's regions in size, it has some big stories to tell. The haunted abandoned Fairfield Hills insane asylum in Newtown achieved cult status after MTV's *Fear* was shot on location there. Hanna Cranna, Monroe's illustrious witch, haunts the graveyard where she's buried. Stratford had its Phelps Mansion, home of the Stratford Knockings, Connecticut's version of the Rochester Rappings in western New York that started the Spiritualist Movement. The Stratford Knockings were even more shocking because of the varied and startling poltergeist activity and the inability of a skeptical public to rebut the phenomenon. Not too far from the former site of Phelps Mansion is the American Shakespeare Festival Theatre, which is also said to be haunted.

Stamford gives us heroes, witches, and bizarre weather phenomena. Its witch trials of 1692 put Salem, Massachusetts, to shame but gave our country hope for our collective humanity, which was badly needed at that trying time. Stamford's residents in particular have been unusually admirable throughout history—even in a world gone awry. At the Stamford witch trials of Goody Clawson and Goody Disborough, wise and just men put their foot down and ended the witch hysteria with one resounding fell swoop. Nearly a hundred years later, on a day marked by unnatural darkness of unknown origin, giving rise to fears that Doomsday was at hand, Stamford resident Abraham Davenport became Connecticut's sweetheart-of-the-moment for remaining calm during the crisis when everyone around him was falling apart. He insisted on manning his post on the Connecticut General Assembly, where he was a councilman, no matter what would or would not come. For that reason, his behavior was deemed as rare and unusual as the Dark Day itself. Easton's Union Cemetery is home to the White Lady of Easton, who is right up there with the state's most famous graveyard ghosts, all of whom seem to be women: the White Lady, the Green Lady, and Hanna Cranna.

The Dark Day

"Immediately after the tribulation of those days shall the sun be darkened, and the moon shall not give her light."—Matthew 24:29–30 (KJV)

May 19, 1780, was a day Connecticut will never forget. Almost as memorable as the startling darkness that encompassed all of New England during daytime hours was the reaction of one esteemed Stamford native, Abraham Davenport. It began a couple weeks earlier, when residents of Connecticut noticed a strange, mustard yellow and red tinge to the atmosphere. Sometimes causing reduced visibility, the curious meteorological phenomenon made silver objects appear the color of brass, and many folks were enchanted by the lovely greenish blue hue the sky cast on their lawns and foliage.

But on that Black Friday, the nineteenth, a complete and utter darkness swept over the land just before noon. Animals instinctively reacted the way they would have at dusk, retiring to their nests and barns. A strange, foreboding eeriness permeated every community as the implications of what many feared was happening began to sink in. Being the God-fearing, Bible-believing people that the devout Puritans of the time were, they truly believed the

Day of Judgment had arrived. After all, the books of Matthew (24:29) and Mark (13:24) both predicted it would happen that way. They prayed by candlelight.

Over in the Old State House in Hartford, the Connecticut General Assembly was in session when the darkness arrived, and the councillors were aware that people were becoming panicked. The House of Representatives adjourned, but the General Assembly asked its members how to proceed under the circumstances. Stamford lawmaker Abraham Davenport replied with a statement, quoted often since that day, as a message to inspire devotion to duty under difficult circumstances: "I am against adjournment. The day of judgment is either approaching, or it is not. If it is not, there is no cause for an adjournment; if it is, I choose to be found doing my duty. I wish therefore that candles may be brought." Deliberations continued that day, and Davenport's famous response made Connecticut proud, inspiring poems, quotes, and even a day of celebration to honor the venerable Davenport and remember Connecticut's Dark Day. President John F. Kennedy used Davenport's words in several of his presidential campaign speeches in 1960, saying he hoped that we as a nation, too, "may bring candles to help light our country's way."

The sunlight finally returned later in the afternoon on that strange Colonial day, while Davenport and the State Senate continued their work. The crisis had been averted, and Davenport's seemly behavior was as big news as the Dark Day itself. Nine years later, Davenport had just presided over a case in Danbury, all the while not feeling well, and the moment he retired to his quarters, he died. In 1868, John Greenleaf Whittier wrote a poem called "Abraham Davenport," which ended with the following verse, describing a mural of Davenport called *Dark Day*, painted by Delos Palmer for the city courtroom:

> And there he stands in memory to this day,
> Erect, self-poised, a rugged face, half seen
> Against the background of unnatural dark,
>   A witness to the ages as they pass,
>   That simple duty hath no place for fear.

As for the circumstances that may have caused the Dark Day, many theories have been suggested over the years, but today we think we know what actually happened. It wasn't Judgment Day. It wasn't a sign of Revelation's Sixth Seal being opened, as predicted in both Matthew and Mark. It was not a solar eclipse, as some learned men of science speculated. Based on scientific analyses of rainwater taken that day and surviving handwritten notes on the findings, we now believe major forest fires to the north of New England released so much ash into the atmosphere that sunlight could not penetrate the particulate matter. The rainwater sampled that day smelled of soot and was tinged a grayish color. It felt grainy, like soot. Since the Dark Day of 1780, other cases of loss of daylight due to forest fires and volcanoes have occurred, but we have the technology to communicate impending bouts of darkness to the public quickly to discourage a repeat of the fear that gripped Connecticut in 1780.

Fairfield Hills

At its peak of business, if you could call it that, the Fairfield State Hospital, now known as Fairfield Hills and belonging to the Town of Newtown, housed about four thousand allegedly insane people in a vast complex of buildings that are largely abandoned except for those housing government offices. The institution had a history of performing experimental shock treatment and lobotomies in its day. Maybe that explains the phantom screams once reported emanating from buildings and tunnels vacated since the 1990s. Fairfield is credited with having been the first place to perform a lobotomy to treat mental illness in the United States. Not surprisingly, because of its controversial and unprecedented medical practices, it also had a history of mysterious deaths.

Like many institutions of this type, it has a series of underground tunnels leading from one building to the next, and those tunnels are said to be quite haunted. They pose a grave threat to intruders and ghost hunters, however, because of severe deterioration and the threat of imminent collapse. The entire complex has become so unstable, in fact, that many of the buildings are now set for demolition. For safety reasons alone, the Town of Newtown and the Fairfield Hills Management Committee, which manages the property, rightfully take security very seriously. Several armed police cars roam the property continuously, keeping trespassers at bay. Even though it is illegal to enter the property after dark, the police still have their hands full, thanks to the 1996 hit movie *Sleepers*, which was filmed there, and MTV's *Fear*, which aired an episode shot on site. Fairfield Hills' nearly legendary status as a haunted site is proliferated online, as it is listed in virtually every compilation of haunted Connecticut sites on the Internet. The claim is that there have been sightings of a petite young woman in white, surrounded by a glow, staring through the windows of the abandoned buildings. A nurse? A patient? We'll never know. Apparently she has eluded capture by local law enforcement.

Hanna Cranna

Nobody knows for certain when Hanna Hovey became the more poetic Hanna Cranna. I doubt it was her maiden name. After her husband, Captain Joseph Hovey, died a very suspicious death in the early 1800s, the Monroe villagers started wondering if perhaps Hanna were a witch. According to Hanna at the time, the good Captain awoke one morning and went for his customary walk. Only he apparently became disoriented somehow and walked right off a cliff, plunging to his death. He was in his prime, and it made no sense that he would just walk straight off a cliff, so people began to whisper that Hanna had cast a spell on the man; after all, she was the last person to see him before his death.

Well, if they were going to call her a witch, Hanna decided she would really give them something to talk about. She would *become* a witch! After all, she had nothing to lose, but much to gain. Knowing that her neighbors all believed she was a witch anyway, Hanna made it a habit to stop by their homes and scare them into offering her free food and firewood, just to get her to leave. But her manner soon turned even more brazen, as she demanded the best food from any chosen household, not just the humble offerings typically provided. One farmer's wife dared to deny Hanna the largest pie on her table—the farmer's favorite—instead offering a much smaller one to the witch. Hanna left in a huff and must have cast an evil spell on the woman, because it was said the farmer's wife was never able to bake again. A similar fate befell a fisherman caught fishing on Hanna's property. After she scolded him and threw him off her land, he was never able to fish again.

On the other hand, those who believed in Hanna's impressive abilities were duly rewarded. For example, one farmer approached her, pleading for help in getting rain for his dying crop. She could sense his sincerity and need, so she told him he would get his rain precisely at midnight. At the stroke of twelve, the rain began, ending a weeks-long drought. But those who would jest at the woman, who perhaps was becoming a little too comfortable in her witch role, paid the price. Two men once approached Hanna for a favor, but they couldn't hide their smirks as they spoke to her, so she told them what they wanted to hear and sent them merrily on their way. As they rode off, their smirks turning into outright belly laughs, the wheels suddenly fell off their wagon and they lost their oxen. No doubt, as they walked the rest of the way home, they had plenty of time to think about what they'd done.

Hanna lived on top of Craig Hill in the Bug Hill–Cutler's Farm section of Monroe, in a house said to be guarded by snakes of every type and size. There was also her pet rooster, Old Boreas, whom some believed was actually her "familiar," a spirit said to take the form of an animal and assist witches in their activities. All real witches were believed to have them. Old Boreas crowed at midnight each night with such precision that neighbors could set their clocks by it. No spring chick herself, Hanna knew her own time was near when the rooster died. She buried Old Boreas at exactly midnight. She told a trusted neighbor the following morning that she would soon die and wished to have her coffin carried by foot, not by wagon, to the cemetery. Of that, she was adamant.

She died the next day, but unfortunately, a snowstorm hampered efforts to carry her casket through the knee-deep snow. The pallbearers decided instead to load the casket onto a wagon. What were they thinking? You don't deny a witch her dying wish. The casket rolled off the wagon and slid halfway down Craig Hill. Again the men loaded it onto the wagon, securing it with the weight of two men sitting on top of the casket, but then it began vibrating so strongly that the men finally chose to honor Hanna's wish and carry her casket by foot all the way to the cemetery. When they finished their grim task and headed back to town, they learned that Hanna's house had gone up in flames shortly after they took her body away from it.

Now, at least once a year, a driver passing by Stepney Cemetery swerves to avoid a woman in the middle of the road, who he or she later learns was a ghost, and crashes into the same tombstone—that of Hanna Cranna. The Town of Monroe replaces the marker almost annually. Hanna always knew how to stir things up like that.

Phelps Mansion

Phelps Mansion was a three-story dwelling in Stratford built by Captain George Dowell in 1826. In 1849, Dowell sold the house at 1738 Elm Street to Dr. Eliakim Phelps. Phelps was a Presbyterian minister from Philadelphia with a penchant for the mysterious and unknown. Caught up in the hype of the Spiritualist Movement, he was known to hold séances at his new house. One séance in particular may have opened a can of worms—or perhaps something much larger, like, say, a spirit portal—that would torment generations in the home, until it was finally demolished and turned into a parking lot in 1972.

As far as anyone can tell, it began on March 4, 1850, when Phelps and an old friend who was visiting got into a discussion about the Spiritualist Movement and whether it could really be possible to contact the "other side." To settle it, they held an impromptu séance—just the two of them. At the time, their efforts seemed to produce only a few unexplainable knocks and raps. With such pitiable feedback from the spirit world, they were left uncertain as to whether they had actually gotten through. Six days later, Phelps received an unequivocal answer to that matter. The day that went down in history for what became known as the Stratford Knockings was March 10, 1850.

That morning, Phelps and his young wife and children went to mass, as usual. But while they were away, someone was at play back at the mansion. When the family returned home, they discovered the previously locked front door wide open, with a black cloth draped over it, as if to suggest mourning. Upon entering the house, they found total disarray. It looked as if the house had been ransacked, and that might have been their first inclination, were it not for the horrifying site on their dining-room table. There, for a fleeting moment, they saw an apparition of a woman laid out across the table, as if on display for a wake. Then she vanished before their eyes. Some believe it was the ghost of Goody Bassett, an alleged witch hanged on that very property in 1661—the third to be hanged in New England.

Phelps sent his wife and children out and had the police come in to investigate. No sign of forced entry was found, no objects of value were missing—not even cash that had been lying out in plain view—and no trace of an intruder could be found. Their house had been invaded, but by whom . . . or what? Over the course of the day, and indeed the next few days and weeks, the unexplained and horrifying became commonplace at the Phelps home. Strange rappings could be heard within the walls and doors themselves, and objects were often moved, sometimes thrown across a room, and other times slowly levitating before unbelieving eyes. Silverware was found bent or broken, and the children were assaulted by unseen hands, often in plain view of witnesses. Some of the family members found their clothing stuffed into lifelike positions on their beds and arranged with hands crossed over the chest, as a body would be positioned in a casket.

One of the most astonishing phenomena was the placement of very lifelike stuffed figures, made from Mrs. Phelps's clothing, in ritualistic poses. But these figures were created by unseen hands at an inhuman speed and somehow teleported through the house while nobody was watching. It started out with eleven such figures and eventually reached thirty in number. This even occurred while investigators were on guard. It was humanly impossible to create and place that many figures that quickly in another room without someone noticing, and yet it happened repeatedly.

Word of the poltergeist activity at Phelps Mansion spread rapidly, and Dr. Phelps didn't mind accommodating those who believed it was some kind of a hoax. He invited in the naysayers as well as the supporters and anyone who might be able to help. Reporters, investigators, priests, and friends all paid the mansion a visit, and all walked away certain that whatever was happening there was very real.

Various theories were offered for the paranormal activity. Some, of course, believed it was all a hoax, without ever visiting the house. Others, including Phelps, were inclined to think it was the work of an evil spirit. And still others noticed a correlation between the activity and the presence of two of the children. When those two children were sent to boarding school, the activity in the house was greatly, if not entirely, reduced.

A prevalent current theory on poltergeist activity is that it is often associated with prepubescent children in the home. Remove the children and you eliminate the problem. The children do not consciously manipulate objects in their environment, but somehow their energy disperses into the atmosphere unchecked, and through some form of subconscious telekinesis, everything around them goes crazy. It's a popular theory, but not necessarily my own. What would account for the apparition seen on the dining-room table? And why did a nursing home that was opened years later in the house experience paranormal activity? And we mustn't forget that Phelps invited spirits into his home with his séances. Perhaps it was a combination of poltergeist activity caused by the children's presence and the troublemaking spirits Dr. Phelps invited into his home when he held the séance.

In the fall of 1850, after months of torment and public ridicule, the family moved back to Philadelphia, at least for the winter. When they returned to their Stratford home the following summer, the activity that had plagued them the year before had ceased. For the remainder of their time there, nothing out of the ordinary happened to the Phelps family in their mansion, whether or not the children were home.

In 1947, the home was turned into a convalescent nursing home, and the paranormal activity that had been blessedly dormant for nearly a hundred years was somehow reawakened. Don't tell me it was from all of the energy of the senior citizens! The owner of the nursing home had an infant son who apparently had somebody "up there" watching over him. On at least two occasions, someone sounded the buzzer next to his crib in his third-floor bedroom, alerting her to imminent danger that threatened her son's life. It was the only perk of living in a haunted house. The rest of the staff wasn't keen about the whispering they heard beside them when nobody was there or seeing heavy doors swing open and slam shut without visible assistance. Such inexplicable incidents in the nursing home continued until 1968, when the mansion was finally abandoned. Three years later, however, police responding to a report of vandalism on the property chased a young girl they saw to the third floor, but they never found her. She disappeared without a trace. Maybe it was one of the Phelps girls returning home, or perhaps it was another stray spirit who came through the portal Dr. Phelps opened on that fateful day in 1850.

In 1972, the house was demolished to make room for a parking lot. All paranormal activity has presumably ceased, but if you park there one day and hear someone knocking on your car door, beware of the Stratford poltergeist!

The Shakespeare Theatre

Not far from the site of the old Phelps Mansion, home of the famous Stratford Knockings, is the American Shakespeare Festival Theatre at Stratford (Shakespeare Theatre for short), which is said to be haunted by actors of the nineteenth and early twentieth centuries. Stage ropes swing when nobody has pushed them, and phantom laughter has been heard. Paranormal investigators have listened to ethereal voices talking and crying and have captured spirit energy in various forms on film.

The theater complex stands at 1850 Elm Street, on the site of some of Stratford's earliest settlers' homes. Its administration building, the "white house" at the entrance to the grounds, was built in 1785. A detached building in the rear of the complex was a kitchen used to serve soldiers during the Revolutionary War. However, the theater section itself wasn't constructed until 1954. In June 1951, the Connecticut General Assembly established the American Shakespeare Festival Theatre as a nonprofit educational corporation to expose students to Shakespearean works, and the remainder of the complex was constructed beginning in 1954. In 1955, the theater opened with a performance of *Julius Caesar*, and at one time or another, it hosted such stars as Roddy McDowall, Katharine Hepburn, Ed Asner, Hal Holbrook, and Helen Hayes.

Eventually other theaters opened, and many of the big names started going elsewhere. The Shakespeare Theatre's plays were not drawing the crowds they once did, and the property was sold to the state in 1983. In the 1990s, a series of unfortunate incidents, including problems with lighting, faulty air-conditioning, trash, traffic, theft, and even mysterious medical crises of some performers, gave the theater some bad publicity and caused a heavy financial burden. Worse, a man was stabbed to death in 1995 on the grounds, and rumors had it that a young lady had been raped and murdered on the site and an old man was found frozen to death at the theater. These last two stories are unsubstantiated, but reports of ghostly phenomena make you wonder if there were, indeed, restless spirits on the grounds. An apparition of a woman had been seen in the upstairs windows of the administration building, electronic equipment malfunctioned regularly, and many photographs revealed psychic energy.

On February 8, 2005, the State of Connecticut transferred the theater's deed to the Town of Stratford. The nonprofit organization currently is closed to the public while the town reorganizes efforts to reopen the theater. The Department of Community/Economic Development is considering bids by qualified candidates for the redevelopment of the once-thriving theater. It will be interesting to see who or what is awakened when the theater is revived.

The Stamford Witch Trials

"Thou shalt not suffer a witch to live."—Exodus 22:18 (KJV)

The year 1692 was a bad one for witches. The disastrous events surrounding the Salem witch trials in Massachusetts left a bad taste that continues to linger to this day, centuries later. But for all the misery of that regrettable time, a witch trial in Stamford that ran concurrently with the Salem fiasco gave cause for hope in the human condition.

Stamford's witch hunt was not unlike others in old New England. As in Salem, a child's false accusations started a chain of events that affected an entire community. Katherine "Kate" Branch, a conniving seventeen-year-old maidservant of Daniel Wescot, was probably afflicted by epilepsy, but perhaps afraid she'd be accused of being a witch herself, she fabricated a tale that placed blame for her then-unexplainable fits of seizures and hallucinations on the work of two women, whom she alleged were the true witches. Though the mistress of the house, Abigail Wescot, could see right through the girl's tale, Mr. Wescot took the young servant's side, as did many of the townsfolk. Thankfully, however, justice prevailed when the judges hearing the case ultimately came to their good senses, setting a precedent that put an end to the witch hysteria, at least in Connecticut colony . . . and put Miss Branch in her rightful place.

Witchcraft in early New England was a capital offense, based on Old English and religious precedents. In 1642, Connecticut passed a law stating, "If any man or woman be a witch—that is, hath or consulteth with a familiar spirit—they shall be put to death." The key was to prove witchcraft. Before the incident at Stamford in 1692, ten people had been convicted of witchcraft in Connecticut between 1647 and 1662. Four of the accused were put to death. Belief in witchcraft was widespread in the New England colonies of the seventeenth century, paving the way for an epidemic of fear. Much of that fear and prejudice came to a grinding halt following the Salem witch trials in 1692, when observers from neighboring colonies saw the havoc such toxic intolerance could wreak on entire communities. By the time of the Stamford witch hunt and trials, nobody had been executed for practicing witchcraft in thirty years, at least in Connecticut. But that didn't ease the tension in Stamford during the prolonged trials of Goody Clawson and Goody Disborough, who barely escaped the death sentence in 1693.

Their story didn't receive as much publicity as the Salem witch trials, but it should have, if for no other reason than the sheer difference in outcome of the trials. It is well documented today, however, by Ronald Marcus of the Stamford Historical Society in a paper he wrote in 1976 called, "Elizabeth Clawson . . . Thou Deseruest to Dye," and by Richard Godbeer in his book *Escaping Salem: The Other Witch Hunt of 1692.*

As the story goes, servant girl Kate Branch was suspected of being bewitched by several local alleged witches soon after she began suffering spells, which included seizures, hallucinations, hearing voices and seeing people nobody else could see, seeing bright lights, a sensation of pins and needles, and swallowing her tongue. Today we know all these to be signs of epilepsy, but back then, in the midst of the witch hysteria, with a young woman specifically naming women who were allegedly trying to do her in, the most likely cause of the symptoms was believed to be witchcraft.

Kate was lucky, as far as servants go. Her master and mistress were wealthy, and she lived a comfortable life working for them. The last thing she would want would be to jeopardize her job with them and be cast out on the streets for some bizarre ailment she'd become afflicted with that couldn't be explained. Rather than risk losing her job and the life she'd grown accustomed to, and realizing that the attacks were increasing in intensity and frequency and could no longer be hidden, Kate may have consciously chosen to blame it on a couple of women she knew her masters didn't get along with. Or maybe she truly believed she was bewitched; it didn't take much to make one believe such a thing in those days. At any rate, Elizabeth Clawson and Mercy Disborough were brought to trial, and the entire community became involved in the outcome.

It didn't matter that the accused adamantly denied any sort of conspiracy with the Devil in afflicting Kate Branch. It didn't really even matter when dozens of courageous neighbors came forth and did something unspeakable in those days to save their friend Elizabeth Clawson, signing an affidavit attesting to her good character and submitting it to the court. Such an act might have caused the court to wonder if they were witches defending one of their own. Instead, it made everyone pause, take a deep breath, and really think about what they were doing, and whether they really wanted a repeat of the mistakes made in Salem. Still, before it was over, both women were subjected to various "witch tests," which seem ridiculous today (and even did then to some men of science and common sense). One test required that the women be examined naked from head to toe by either a physician or midwife, who would look for "Devil's marks," moles or birthmarks that would not bleed when a needle was passed through them by anyone other than the Devil, because they bled only when he partook of a witch's blood. Elizabeth Clawson was found to be without any signs of such Devil's marks; however, Mercy Disborough had several moles that refused to bleed upon probing.

The next so-called tried-and-true witch test used on the two women was the flotation test. Not generally used in the American colonies, determining the buoyancy of people accused of being witches was, at that time, often used in Europe. It involved tying an accused witch's right hand to her left foot and left hand to her right foot, and tossing her into a deep body of water. If she floated, she was truly a witch, because the water would refuse to accept such a being, since water plays such an important part in Christian baptism. But if she sank, she was innocent. And if they didn't pull her back up in time, her proof of innocence was for naught.

This barbaric practice was condemned in the colonies years earlier by the esteemed Increase Mather and other men in power. "This practice has no foundation in nature, nor in Scripture," Mather said. "The Bodies of Witches have not lost their natural properties; they have weight in them as well as others . . . the Scripture does no where appoint any such course to be taken to find out whether persons are in league with the devil or no. It remains, then, that the experiement is diabolical." Diabolical or not, Goody Disborough was so certain she could prove her innocence by being cast "into ye watter" that she requested it be done immediately. Unfortunately, both women bobbed like corks on the surface of the water—proving to the ignorant that they were witches. But even though the testimony regarding that experiment was sworn to in court, the court still had a devil of a time with their decision regarding the fate of the two women.

The trial began with the grand jury returning indictments against both women on September 14, 1692. The findings of the water test were submitted and accepted by the court as evidence, as was sworn testimony of witnesses who had seen Kate Branch cry out the names of the accused during the fits she suffered almost daily now. However, the testimony of individuals who believed Elizabeth Clawson was innocent, including the affidavit signed by twenty-six people who knew her, was also accepted by the court for consideration. Deliberation over the evidence was long, and the jury was unable to reach a consensus, so the court agreed to seek assistance from the higher general court in October. The prisoners were returned to jail, and the jurors were told to be available to the general court when called upon.

The following month, a group of prominent ministers was given all of the evidence to go over so it could submit a formal opinion to the general court. The ministers made four points, according to Marcus in his paper regarding the trial. They said that they, too, believed that conviction based on the sink-or-swim method was "unlawful, sinful, and therefore it cannot afford any evidence." They further stated that only an able physician, not a woman without medical background, could determine whether "Devil's marks" found on prisoner's bodies should be used as evidence. They believed some of young Kate's testimony to be questionable and perhaps false, and they determined that she might have a medical affliction, not unlike her own mother's condition, that was responsible for her strange experiences. They topped off these carefully considered points with the admonition that they found the strange accidents ascribed to the accused "as matters of witchcraft to be upon very slender & uncertain ground."

After careful review of the ministers' official stand and other evidence presented in the case, the general court jury still was unable to agree on a verdict. The governor stepped in and told the court to reconvene as soon as possible to reach a verdict. When the court reconvened, additional testimony was presented, and the jury quickly found Mercy Disborough guilty as charged. The court approved it, and the governor sentenced her to death. Elizabeth Clawson was found not guilty, thanks in part to her friends and her lack of "Devil's marks" on her body. She returned to Stamford and lived until 1714, dying at age eighty-three.

In Mercy's defense, a group representing her petitioned the general court shortly after the trial, claiming that the trial had been illegal because one of the jurors told to "be available" when called before the general court didn't show up. The general court responded by appointing three gentlemen to examine the records of the trial and make a final determination in the matter. In May 1693, the men told the general court that they doubted the validity of the evidence presented against Mercy Disborough, and they reprieved her. Obviously not happy with the ongoing nonsense, they ended their report to the general court much as the meeting of ministers had, with a strong word of caution against any further witch hysteria: "The miserable toil they are in in the Bay for adhering to those last mentioned litigious things is warning enough that those that would make witchcraft of such things would make hanging work apace." Thankfully, the good men of Stamford finally came to their senses, and so marked the beginning of the end of the New England witch hysteria.

Union Cemetery

Easton's Union Cemetery, which dates back to the 1600s, is touted as one of the most famous haunted cemeteries not only in Connecticut, but in the entire United States. In fact, an esteemed pair of Connecticut ghostbusters, Ed and Lorraine Warren, even wrote a book primarily about their experiences at Union Cemetery, called *Graveyard.* Like many others, the Warrens saw the White Lady of

Easton and captured her essence on film. Dozens of people have seen her apparition over the past sixty years, including police officers and firemen. She has long, dark hair and wears what looks like a white nightgown and a white bonnet. The White Lady usually appears in the roadway of Route 59, often being "hit" by vehicles when she appears out of nowhere. But she is never found after the fact, nor is there ever any damage to the vehicles that pass through the mournful woman . . . except in the case of a fireman who had a particularly vivid encounter with her.

He was driving his pickup somewhere between Union Cemetery and Stepney Graveyard, which is ten miles away, when the road in front of him took on a strange reddish glow. In those few surreal seconds, he saw a farmer with a straw hat sitting beside him and a lady in white approaching in the roadway with her hands reaching out toward him. He slammed on the brakes, but it was too late. He heard the thud and even ended up with a dent from the impact, yet no trace of the woman, or the farmer who had been sitting beside him, was ever found. The fact that he heard and was left with physical evidence of the impact is most unusual in cases of cars driving through or into apparitions.

Others never see the woman but hear a woman sobbing. Some believe she is a woman who died during childbirth and is searching eternally for her lost infant. Ed Warren felt it was a woman killed following her husband's murder and funeral in the 1940s near Easton. Some witnesses have seen shadowy figures grabbing at the woman. Perhaps they were thugs who came after her in life after killing her husband. Others wonder if it's Ellen Smathers, whom the Warrens described as the victim of a stalker who first killed her husband in hopes that she would fall in love with the killer. Her husband's body was found in a sinkhole behind the Baptist church near the cemetery. Still another woman was murdered by her adulterous lover in the early 1900s. Her body, too, was found in a sinkhole in the woods near the cemetery.

Given the choice, you might prefer to see the forlorn White Lady rather than the Red-Eyed Creature from the Woods, which also has been reported at Union Cemetery. One poor soul was walking past the cemetery when he caught a glimpse of a pair of red eyes in the brush peering at him through the darkness. As he ran from the sight, he heard footsteps following him, which made him run even faster until he was well away from the cemetery. Cosmic Society's Donna Kent speculates that it was the specter of Earle Kellog, a man who was set afire across the street and burned to death in 1935, or a man, killed by a drunken driver, who provided his name—and a number of choice expletives—to a group of boys trying to capture EVP (electronic voice phenomenon) in the cemetery one night.

The cemetery is located at the junction of Routes 136 and 59, adjacent to the Easton Baptist Church. Access to the cemetery is strictly forbidden from dusk till dawn, and trespassers will be—and have been, in multitudes—arrested and fined. There's a reason why so many old tombstones say "R.I.P." Some things are better left undisturbed.

Central Connecticut

CENTRAL CONNECTICUT IS ALSO KNOWN AS RIVER VALLEY, BECAUSE THE Connecticut River—the largest river in New England—flows straight through the state in this region, from Long Island Sound through the Greater Hartford area, all the way up to the Canadian border. That's why there is such diversity in the overall landscape of Central Connecticut: big-city sophistication (Hartford is the state capital), rolling valleys, sparkling rivers, and charming New England countryside. Sounds like your typical state tourism commercial, but there's something the commercials won't tell you about Central Connecticut: It has a history of witchcraft, paranormal creatures, ghosts, demons, and aliens.

The Benton Homestead in Tolland is called "the most occupied unoccupied building in the state," and for good reason. The Black Dog of Death in Meriden causes people to die tragically after their third chance encounter with it. Canton's Headless Horseman might be able to rest in peace now, since he has finally been identified. Devil's Hopyard is responsible for many a fabled legend about Haddam's witches, both good and bad, and the Devil himself, who, of course, is always bad! The Gay City ghost town of Bolton has a history of strange supernatural occurrences. Water from the Gay City State Park is now a popular swimming hole, but it was once said to flow uphill, which goes against natural law.

The so-called Moodus Noises around Mount Tom were a source of speculation for centuries, but we think we finally know what causes them—we just don't know how or why. Bolton's Notch Hollow has something going on that we can't explain either. Car windows have been reported to mist or fog up as they pass over the defunct railroad tracks at the notch, no matter what the outside temperature is. Is it the steam of a phantom train, the cold breath of a ghost on a warm day, or some sort of freakish weather anomaly? I'd be a bit hesitant to step out of my car and investigate that one. Hartford's Old State House, the nation's oldest State Capitol building, is haunted. Simsbury's Pettibone Tavern, now a steak and seafood restaurant, is gloriously famous for its ghost of Abigail, but even more frightening are the murder and mayhem that occurred there the moment Abigail presumably turned into a ghost. Its haunted ladies' room justifies women going to the bathroom in pairs!

Westbrook is the site of phantom plane crashes and other unexplainable aerial phenomena. It's also the tragic location of the TWA Flight 800 crash in Moriches Bay in 1996, the cause of which was as controversial as the green orbs seen over the water to this day. There also have been reports of little green men in UFOs. The Mary Starr encounter in Old Saybrook in 1957 is one of the most famous Connecticut "close encounters," part of the wave of UFO sightings sweeping over our country during that decade.

The Benton Homestead

Someone once quipped that the Benton Homestead in Tolland is "the most occupied unoccupied building in the state." And the Department of Economic Development must agree, as its *Connecticut Vacation Guide* calls the homestead "a celebrated 'ghost' house." Why all the notoriety? Because, according to *Legendary Connecticut*, a female apparition in a wedding gown has been seen or heard sobbing. Men's voices have also been heard in the unoccupied basement, and a Hessian soldier's spirit has been seen at least once. A general feeling of sadness and oppression sometimes overcomes sensitive individuals who visit the house-turned-museum.

Built in 1720 by Daniel Benton, the Colonial-style Cape Cod has an unusual and poignant history, especially from the Revolutionary War era. Daniel Benton had three grandsons living with him who served in the war. Two died during imprisonment by the British, and the third, twenty-four-year-old Elisha, was sent to a prison ship in New York Harbor, where he contracted deadly smallpox from contaminated blankets before a prisoner exchange with the enemy freed him. In his sickly state, he was turned over to his grandfather's estate to await his imminent death. But nobody else in the Benton family had ever been exposed to smallpox, so they were unwilling to care for their dying relative. However, his beloved seventeen-year-old girlfriend, whom the Benton family had forbidden him to marry, stepped forward without hesitation and offered to go into isolation in a room set aside for that purpose. Jemima Brown cared for Elisha lovingly for three weeks, until his death. Five weeks later, she succumbed to the same ailment.

The Bentons, probably more than a little ashamed of their own attitude toward the couple, were grateful to the courageous girl and humbled by her selfless act of humanity. Although they couldn't make right the desires of the two who had wished so badly to share a life together, at least they could bury them near each other, albeit separated by the carriage house driveway, as traditional custom of the time did not permit unwed couples to be buried side by side. In death, as in life, the couple was destined to be kept apart.

The Benton Homestead was also used to lodge two dozen Hessian soldiers in 1777 as they were traveling across Connecticut toward Boston, where they would be shipped to Germany. But they were said to so enjoy their stopover in Tolland, and at the Benton Homestead specifically, that some are believed to have never left when the rest of the Hessians moved on. I say that in both a physical and spiritual sense, for some Hessian soldiers allegedly settled into the Tolland community with local maidens, and others are believed to now haunt the homestead. One has been seen on the front steps, and ethereal voices have been heard in the basement where Hessian soldiers enjoyed a comfortable stay; so comfortable that they have returned to a place they fondly remember.

As for the female apparition seen wearing a wedding gown, it's quite possibly Jemima, still longing for a wedding day that will never come, still sobbing for the love that eluded her during her short time on earth.

The Tolland Historical Society now owns and operates the Benton Homestead as a museum. Members of the historical society, tour guides, visitors, and neighbors alike have tales to tell about their experiences involving paranormal activity at the Benton Homestead: little footsteps, the sound of a crackling fire in the fireplace when no fire is burning, pets behaving stranger than usual, and so on. At the Benton Homestead, life goes on . . . even when it's over.

Black Dog of Meriden

"And if a man shall meet the black dog once, it shall be for joy; the second time, it shall be for sorrow; and the third, he shall die." This ominous phrase echoes throughout the communities surrounding Meriden in the Hanging Hills of Central Connecticut. With every mysterious tragedy befalling experienced hikers, the elders nod their heads knowingly . . . it was the Black Dog.

Throughout history, all over the world, legends of black dogs associated with impending death abound. Sometimes called Hell Hounds, these malevolent, supernatural creatures are often reported in or around cemeteries, as if guarding the dead or being harbingers of death. Though typical Black Dogs of Death are large, vicious-looking canines with red eyes, the fabled Black Dog that has haunted West Peak in Meriden since at least the 1800s is small and friendly-looking—at least in the first encounter. One person who lived to tell about it said its color was washed-out black, resembling a worn-out, old black felt hat. As is typical with this kind of unexplained phenomena, the Black Dog of Meriden barks silently and appears out of the blue, disappearing just as mysteriously.

It is said that the first time people encounter the little Black Dog in the Hanging Hills near West Peak, good fortune will come to the person who sees it. The second time they encounter the same pooch, they will become ill or suffer from some relatively minor mishap. After the third time they see it, they will suffer a great tragedy, usually their own death. The most recent tragedy occurred on Thanksgiving Day in 1972, when an experienced young climber fell to his death off West Peak in the shadows of Hanging Hills. According to David Philips in *Legendary Connecticut,* at least six deaths have been blamed on triple encounters with the Black Dog.

The most famous account of the legend took place in 1898, as told by W. H. C. Pynchon, a New York City geologist with a fondness for the Hanging Hills and their odd geological formations.

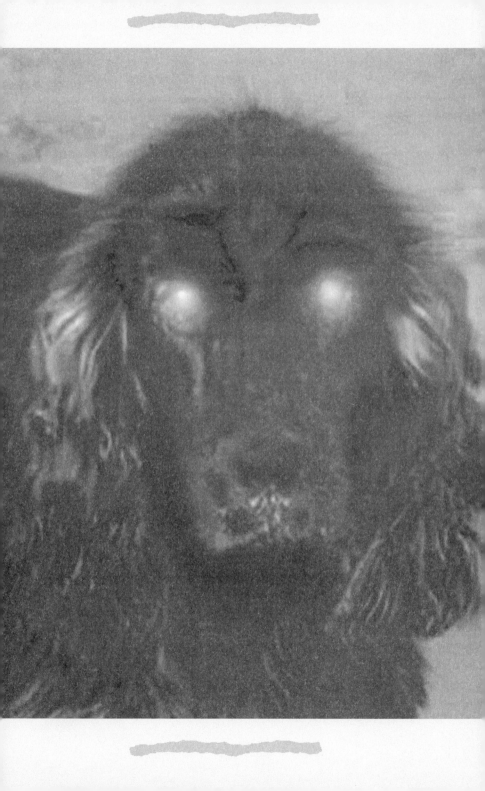

Pynchon's first encounter with the Black Dog was benign enough. The little dog kept him company and made his trek over the West Peak more enjoyable. But as Pynchon made his way back that day, he turned to see that the dog was no longer following him, although he could have sworn he saw a black shadow slinking into the woods behind him. Though he was aware of the legend of the Black Dog of West Peak, the dog he encountered seemed much too friendly to be considered suspect. Besides, usually so-called Black Dogs of Death are described as a large Labrador breed with angry red eyes. Pynchon's canine acquaintance was petite and not the truest black shade. Its sad, spaniel-like eyes belied its obvious friendly temperament, if its wagging tail during that first encounter was any indication of its mood. Surely such a happy-go-lucky creature could not be responsible for the monstrosities attributed to a particular black dog on that mountain.

Several years later, Pynchon returned to Meriden, bringing along a fellow geologist who had climbed West Peak several times. His friend had seen a black dog in that area on two occasions already but thought nothing of silly legends. As the two men began their ascent, Pynchon said that a verse from the Twenty-third Psalm came to mind out of the blue, perhaps because of their stark surroundings while climbing between two cliffs—or perhaps it was a premonition, or a telepathic communication between man and dog. "Yea, though I walk through the valley of the shadow of death . . ." The climbers were on the last leg of their climb when they both spotted the little dog they'd seen before, wagging his tail and barking soundlessly from the highest ledge on the peak. It was Pynchon's second encounter with the dog and his friend's third. Just then, Pynchon's companion lost his footing and plunged to his death several hundred feet below.

That was the last time Pynchon gave a personal account of the legend to anyone. There would be no final chapter—at least not one written by him. Determined to challenge the horrific legend of the Black Dog, to which so many believed his friend had fallen victim, he set out a few years later to retrace the route he and his friend had followed that ill-fated day. . . . Nobody knew for sure whether Pynchon saw the mysterious black dog a third time, but almost everyone in those parts believes he did. His broken and frozen body was discovered in almost the exact same spot as his friend's.

Canton's Headless Horseman

When the Hosford Tavern in Canton burned to the ground more than a hundred years ago, a gruesome discovery in the ashes settled the mystery of the missing Revolutionary War paymaster and subsequent Headless Horseman sightings along the Hartford-Albany turnpike and Canton's rural roads.

In 1777, a French horseman was charged with the task of delivering a month's pay to the French officers at Saratoga. The last time he was seen alive was at the Hosford Tavern, as he walked up the stairs to his room after an evening of socializing with the other patrons over a few drinks, carrying the saddlebags filled with gold and silver he'd been entrusted to deliver the next day. Though the tavern owner, with sweat on his brow, swore he had seen the man depart bright and early in the morning, he was nowhere to be found, and there was no reason to believe he had ever left the place. The investigation was thorough—after all, not only was a man missing, but a lot of people were counting on the pay he had disappeared with. No trace of the man or money was ever found . . . until the Hosford Tavern burned to the ground.

In the ashes was discovered a headless skeleton. With that finding came renewed speculation that the tavern owner had killed the paymaster after seeing the opportunity of acquiring instant wealth and buried him somewhere in the tavern. It also explains the many reports over the years of a headless phantom riding hastily out of town toward Saratoga, as if to make up for lost time. To this day, drivers still report veering off the road to avoid a collision with a semitransparent Headless Horseman, his long, black cape flowing behind him on a darkened stretch of Canton's rural roads.

Devil's Hopyard

In *Myths and Legends of Our Own Land: Tales of Puritan Land* Charles Skinner wrote: "In Devil's Hopyard was a massive oak that never bears leaves or acorns, for it has been enchanted since the time that one of the witches, in the form of a crow, perched on the topmost branch, looked to the four points of the compass, and flew away. That night the leaves fell off, the twigs shriveled, sap ceased to run, and moss began to beard its skeleton limbs."

The massive oak Skinner described in 1896 must surely be gone by now, but the colorful legends surrounding Devil's Hopyard—especially the origination of its name—have endured. Devil's Hopyard in East Haddam is a densely wooded, 860-acre state park featuring caverns, cliffs, Eight Mile River, Chapman's Falls, and a pool of water below the falls filled with mysterious potholes. These geological features are all woven into the legends of how the Hopyard got its name. One says that Satan enjoyed a perch atop the sixty-foot-high Chapman Falls—the crown jewel of the state park—where a sign today reads, "Let the Water Do the Falling."

Early settlers, who believed the Devil was around every corner, suspected that the potholes below the falls had been formed by Satan's hooves. They said he bored holes into the bedrock after he became upset over his tail getting wet in the pool of water and stomped around in a tantrum. You'd think the cool water would have felt refreshing to someone accustomed to such heat! Today we know that perfectly cylindrical potholes beneath waterfalls are formed by stones flowing into eddies with the current and becoming entrapped, spinning forcefully for so long in the same spot that they wear a hole into the stone. When one stone wears down to nothing, another slips into the hole and repeats the process, enlarging the potholes to various sizes.

Another reason for the "Devil" in Devil's Hopyard comes from a different story. A Mullington minister had two sons, one good and one bad. The bad son received frequent beatings from his exasperated teacher for his transgressions. Eventually he was imprisoned for stealing from the church, much to the horror of his father. Shortly after the son's release from jail, the father realized the one-year incarceration had done little to change his son's evil ways, so he kicked the boy out of his home. The son sought refuge at a neighbor's house, where he met a Cuban who asked the young man if he'd like to accompany him to Havana. As a parting joke, the two thought up a plan to make the townspeople, especially the boy's minister father, believe that he had finally been taken away by Satan, just as they'd always predicted he would be. They borrowed a bull's hide complete with horns from the neighbor's home, and the Cuban wrapped it around himself so he would look like the Devil, at least at quick glance. Both men then climbed onto the wagon and sped past the minister's house, with the minister's son screaming as if he were being taken away against his will, and the Cuban Devil laughing hysterically beside him.

The "Hopyard" portion of the name is a bit easier to explain. A malt house once existed on Hopyard Road, with hops flourishing right at the spot now known as Devil's Hopyard. But I have to confess that when I first heard the name, I pictured the Devil hopping about the place, especially in the pool beneath the falls as he created the potholes.

Gay City Ghost Town

Settled in 1796 by a "spirited" religious sect in a league of its own, Gay City lies to the south of the town of Bolton in New London County. All that remains today are a few crumbling stone foundations, cellar holes, the ruins of an old mill, and a handful of tombstones. But a state park was named in its honor in 1953, and the Gay City State Park's favored swimming hole was once a pond built to collect water that—amazingly—flowed uphill.

Elijah Andrus and about thirty hardy followers founded the Gay City site and set to work immediately putting up frame houses in the dark gorge that would at first be called Factory Hollow. Against all odds, though they were isolated from outside assistance, the early settlers built on rocky soil and steep terrain. No wonder the men turned to drinking at least twice a week prior to their compulsory religious services. But the encouragement of alcoholic intake led to drunken brawls and regrettable words, and it wasn't long before some of the first families packed up and moved away, including the founder.

When Andrus left in 1800, John Gay was appointed president of the colony, and Henry Sumner became the spiritual leader. But even though both men were leaders of the community, their families behaved like the Hatfields and the McCoys. Let's just say it was not a cordial relationship. They managed to overcome their differences long enough to come up with a plan for the survival of their faltering settlement in 1804, when they built a wool mill downstream from Still Pond. During construction of the mill, one of the workmen laid his tools down and walked off the job for good when he saw that the water in the channel they dug ran uphill to the waterwheel at Still Pond. He was sure it was the work of the Devil, and you can't really blame the poor guy. After all, none of the villagers were exactly Puritanical—in fact, they loved their booze and their brawls, and the words that came out of their mouths were nothing short of blasphemous. The water was going in the wrong direction just as surely as the community was.

Nevertheless, the mill was completed in 1810, and it briefly boosted Gay City's economy, giving the colony's families hope of its survival. But the War of 1812 had a detrimental economic impact on the mill, just as it did on most other businesses of the time. Sumner purchased the mill and operated it until a fire destroyed it in 1830. A few years later, the Sumner family built a new rag-paper mill at the site of the original wool mill, but it too burned to the ground in 1879. And that was the end of Gay City, for other residents had been filtering out of the community steadily since the first big fire, and the Civil War and the natural deaths of the original settlers had further taxed the colony.

Today visitors to the state park occasionally report seeing strange apparitions, such as a skeleton standing over a charcoal pit and a young man running through the woods with his head in his hands, and there may be a good reason for that. According to *Legendary Connecticut,* by David E. Philips, Gay City had a couple of grisly murders in which justice was never served, so there may be a ghost or two walking around with a bone to pick. A well-liked old jewelry peddler was murdered and robbed just before the Civil War began, and his skeleton was found in a charcoal pit on the edge of town. The murderer was never brought to justice, although many speculated that it had to be the village charcoal burner.

Another murder prior to the Civil War was even more gruesome. A teenage boy who worked for the village blacksmith was late for work one day, and when he arrived, his enraged boss slashed him to death with a butcher knife and decapitated him. Even though it was common knowledge that the perpetrator was the blacksmith, he was never brought to trial. Since that day, a ghostly figure has been seen flitting through the woods deftly, as if in a hurry to get somewhere on time. Sometimes, they say, he carries his head in his hands.

Haddam Witches

As far as witches in Colonial New England go, the town of Haddam sure had 'em—right up there with giants and dragons and devils. The place names of the designated various landmarks around the superstitious town included Devil's Hopyard, Devil's Footprint, Giant's Chair, Dragon's Rock, and, of course, Witch Meadows and Witch Woods. Some of those colorful names, such as Devil's Hopyard, are still in use today. But of the alleged supernatural beings most early New Englanders feared—and there were many—the witches were the most loathsome of all. According to Charles M. Skinner in *Myths and Legends of Our Own Land: Tales of Puritan Land*, one stood out among the rest in Haddam:

> Farmers were especially fearful of a bent old hag in a red hood, who seldom appeared before dusk, but who was apt to be found crouched on their doorsteps if they reached home late, her mole-covered cheeks wrinkled with a grin, two yellow fangs projecting between her lips, and a light shining from her eyes that numbed all on whom she looked. On stormy nights she would drum and rattle at windows, and by firelight and candlelight, her face was seen peering through the panes.

Skinner went on to briefly mention the place where witches rubbed shoulders with the Dark One himself at Devil's Hopyard.

> At Chapman Falls, where the attrition of a stream had worn potholes in the rocks, there were meetings of Haddam witches, to the number of a dozen. They brewed poisons in those holes, cast spells, and talked in harsh tongues with the arch fiend, who sat on the brink of the ravine with his tail laid against his shoulder, like a sceptre, and a red glow emanating from his body.

Stories of witches taking the guise of birds, ususally crows, were abundant in the seventeenth century. Typically, no matter where it took place or who was involved, a crow was said to harass its victim, forcing the victim to fight back—usually with a silver bullet, since silver was the only metal believed capable of taking down an evil force. If shot with silver, the bird collapsed, and a nearby hag believed to be a witch would fall at precisely the same moment as the crow, with identical injuries. Skinner offered a classic example in *Tales of a Puritan Land*:

The appearance of witches in the guise of birds was no unusual thing, indeed, and a farmer named Blakesley shot one of them in that form. He was hunting in a meadow when a rush of wings was heard and he saw pass overhead a bird with long neck, blue feathers, and feet like scrawny hands. It uttered a cry so weird, so shrill, so like mocking laughter that it made him shudder. This bird alighted on a dead tree, and he shot at it. With another laughing yell it circled around his head. Three times he fired with the same result. Then he resolved to see if it were uncanny, for nothing evil can withstand silver—except Congress. Having no bullets of that metal, he cut two silver buttons from his shirt and rammed them home with a piece of cloth and a prayer. This time the bird screamed in terror, and tried, but vainly, to rise from the limb. He fired. The creature dropped, with a button in its body, and fell on its right side. At that moment an old woman living in a cabin five miles distant arose from her spinning wheel, gasped, and fell on her right side . . . dead.

Moodus Noises

Long before the first European settlers reached Central Connecticut, the Native American tribes had been witness to strange subsurface rumblings that they both heard and felt around Mount Tom in Moodus. The cause of the sounds has been a source of speculation for centuries, but one thing is certain: The Moodus Noises put the tiny town of Moodus on the map.

The earliest inhabitants of the area from which the sounds emanated were the Mohegans, Narragansetts, and Pequots. Those tribes believed the dreadful sounds came from an evil deity whom they were to appease. They named the land of strange sounds Moodus, meaning "Place of Bad Noises," and called on their medicine men to interpret the sounds that spewed forth from the mountain so that they could attempt to appease the deity by way of ceremony or sacrifice, as determined by their powwows. By the time the first European settlers arrived in the 1670s, the Wangunk Indians were so certain of what they were dealing with that they warned their white brethren about the evil lurking below the surface. When the settlers first heard the startling sounds for themselves, however, they were more inclined to blame the sounds on Satan, who seemed to be in hot water for a lot of natural calamities at the time, rather than the Indian's evil Hobomoko.

According to David E. Philip's *Legendary Connecticut*, Haddam's first minister, the Reverend Steven Hosmer, described the phenomenon to a friend in Boston in 1729:

"An old Indian was asked what was the reason of the noises in this place, to which he replied that the Indian's god was angry because the Englishman's god was come here. Now whether there be anything diabolical in these things, I know not, but this I know, that Almighty God is to be seen and trembled at in what has been often heard among us. Whether it be fire or air distressed in the subterranean caverns of the earth cannot be known, for there is no eruption, no explosion perceptible, but by sounds and tremors which are sometimes very fearful and dreadful."

The reverend believed that the Devil was afoot—or underfoot, I should say—in the very town he was charged with ministering to. Talk about an unfortunate relocation!

Once the idea of Hobomoko or Satan being responsible for the Moodus Noises fizzled out, another typical Colonial-era theory arose: witches. A battle between Haddam's good witches, who practiced white magic, and Moodus's bad witches, who practiced black magic, was being waged deep within the mountain. That idea seemed as good as any other for several decades, until Dr. Steel came on the scene.

According to Charles Skinner, "If the witch fights were continued too long, the king of Machimoddi who sat on a throne of solid sapphire in the cave whence the noises came, raised his wand: then the light of the carbuncle went out, thunder rolled through the rocky chambers, and the witches rushed into the air." Inconceivable as that may seem, equally strange was the legend of Dr. Steel, who hailed from England in the 1760s like a knight in shining armor and seemed to at least temporarily solve the mystery of the Moodus Noises. He came to town proclaiming that he would silence the mountain, and when he left, he seemed to have succeeded. As Skinner described it: "Dr. Steele, a learned and aged man from England, built a crazy-looking house in a lonely spot on Mount Tom and was soon as much a mystery as the noises, for it was known that he had come to this country to stop them by magic and to seize the great carbuncle in the cave—if he could find it. Every window, crack, and keyhole was closed, and nobody was admitted while he stayed there, but the clang of hammers was heard in his house all night."

Eventually, after many nights, Dr. Steele's clanging stopped. If a "carbuncle" was truly responsible for all the ruckus, then Steele must have finally found it, thought the villagers. The strange, brilliant man who allegedly possessed magical powers left town as quietly as he had come, and his departure coincided with the end to the Moodus Noises. Coincidence? Perhaps, if one were to believe latter-day men of science. But the Moodus Noises never again sounded with the ferocity of those years.

With the aid of sophisticated equipment and extensive historical and geophysical research, modern seismologists have attributed the Moodus Noises to shallow microearthquakes. They haven't yet managed, however, to explain how Dr. Steele seemed to control the microearthquakes, if that's what they truly were. Among the other scientific explanations (which always seem to suck the fun out of a good legend) were wind and atmospheric conditions echoing through the caves, even though no evidence was found showing a correlation between the timing of the noises and meteorological conditions. Underground mineral explosions were considered but quickly dismissed, as were underground electromagnetic currents.

Finally, around 1979, seismologists discovered that although the earthquakes had been too small for people even to feel—some being so tiny, in fact, that they had a *negative* measurement on the Richter scale!—tiny earthquakes *had* accompanied the Moodus Noises all along. It was further determined that all of the earthquake activity had occurred in a very small area, deep within the earth, and not on any known fault line. How a minuscule earthquake concentrated in a tiny area five thousand feet beneath the surface could cause such a commotion is anyone's guess. In 1988, geologist Tom Stattan stated the current view in *Science News* magazine: "For reasons not entirely clear, sound passes relatively freely between the ground and the air in Moodus." You think?

Notch Hollow

Notch Hollow is a skeleton of its former self, with just one of the twenty-six buildings that were there during its heyday in 1913 still standing today. It's the proverbial ghost town, where, wouldn't you know it, the only inhabitants are ghosts. Or so they say . . .

From the late 1700s into the early 1900s, Notch Hollow was such an important settlement in Quarryville that the two names were synonymous. For nearly two centuries, quarrying of valuable Bolton granite and flagstone took place in and around Quarryville, which was one of two thriving centers in the town of Bolton in the 1800s. The quarrying created a thirty-foot-deep trench for which the settlement was named. Today, it is more often referred to as Bolton Notch. It became much larger and deeper when a railroad was cut through the Notch from 1847 through 1849, and it was widened again in 1929. The railroad and the quarrying contributed to Quarryville's growth in 1913, when Bolton Notch was thriving. But 1916 marked the beginning of the end, when Connecticut's first four U.S. highways were constructed. By 1952, all but one of the twenty-seven historic homes that had been built in Bolton Notch were destroyed for Route 6 upgrades. That one remains today. Then in 1956, a hurricane washed out a railroad bridge in the area, and the railroad track that put Bolton Notch on the map was laid permanently to rest. Today either Mother Nature is still interfering or a phantom train still haunts its route . . . or both.

According to Hans DePold, town of Bolton historian, strange weather anomalies tend to occur only at the Notch: "Drivers have reported their car windows misting over and sometimes freezing solid white as they pass over the abandoned railroad line in the deepest part of the Notch." A phantom steam engine has been reported several times along the railroad, rolling silently along on rails that are no longer there. Sometimes steam is seen moving across the countryside, as if from an old steam train. Could the steam from a ghost train be responsible for misting up car windows at the Notch today?

DePold also points out that an eerie voice is sometimes heard singing high up on the rocks on warm summer nights and suggests that there are many people who may have reason to haunt the Notch: victims of early quarrying accidents; a young Dutchman who was fatally wounded by colonists in his cave at Bolton Notch after marrying an Indian maiden, which was forbidden at that time; and Chief Miantinomah of the Pequot tribe, who was killed with a tomahawk in 1643 at the conclusion of the Pequot War. The bodies of the last two were never known to be found.

Interestingly, Bolton Notch is flanked by two infamous U.S. highways: Route 44, which goes through the very haunted Rehoboth, Massachusetts, and Route 6, which was listed in 1995 by *Reader's Digest* as the second most dangerous road in America. Perhaps the ghostly Red-Headed Hitchhiker of Rehoboth is hitching a ride to Bolton Notch every now and then and blowing his phantom breath on car windows as they pass by. He always has to have his mug plastered in the window of someone's moving vehicle. Do you have a better explanation?

Old State House

The Old State House at 300 Main Street in Hartford is where it all began for Connecticut. It was on that very spot that, in 1639, the enactment by the English colonists of what is said to be our nation's first written constitution establishing representative government, the Fundamental Orders, took place. This is why Connecticut is called the Constitution State. Though it wasn't the U.S. Constitution, many historians have said it was the basis for that later document. Representatives from around the state met in Hartford that year to establish a government called the Connecticut Colony for their fledgling, and rapidly expanding, settlements. Among other things, the Fundamental Orders placed limitations on the powers of the governor and put into effect more liberal voting requirements.

Thus nearly four centuries of history, shaping both Connecticut and the United States, originated at the site of the Old State House. The Federal-style structure is the nation's oldest State Capitol building. Designed by architect Charles Bulfinch, it opened for business in 1796 and was used as a statehouse until 1878, when the current capitol building was completed—which, by the way, is also said to be haunted. Even with all those years under its belt, and even though it's the site of the first witch hanging in New England in 1647, the Old State House itself is only marginally haunted. But that's okay, because the alleged ghost was a pretty colorful guy, even before he turned into a ghost.

The rumor is that the ghost of Joseph Steward, a local painter and museum keeper, haunts the second floor of the Old State House. In 1796, the year the Old State House opened, Steward requested permission from Governor Wolcott to open a painting studio on the third floor, where he would turn out portraits of Connecticut's famous citizens and hang them throughout the building for all to enjoy. At the same time, the man began collecting unusual objects—much like the nineteenth century's P. T. Barnum—and displaying them in his art studio. In 1797, when Steward realized his customers were more interested in the exotic objects he collected, such as a two-headed calf and a unicorn horn, than his paintings, he opened the Museum of Natural and Other Curiosities on the same floor as his art studio. For 25 cents, visitors could gawk at his bizarre collection on the third floor. But soon his collection became too large to keep in the Old State House, so he moved it across the street, where he continued adding to the collection until his death in 1822.

Because Steward played such an important role in the history of the Old State House two centuries ago, the Old State House Association, a nonprofit association formed in 1975 to protect and preserve the site and building, opened the Old State House Museum of Natural and Other Curiosities in Joseph Steward's memory on the building's second floor. Using diaries and newspaper advertisements from Steward's day, the association was able to locate replicas of many of the items he had in his collection, and it has taken up the challenge of continuing to add pieces felt to be in keeping with Steward's interests. Perhaps that's why his footsteps sometimes can still be heard on the second floor.

Pettibone Tavern

Built in 1780, the Pettibone Tavern was a roadside inn that served as a stagecoach stop on the Boston-Albany turnpike. After a series of unfortunate incidents over the course of many years, it became the Chart House Restaurant. Today the historic steak-and-seafood restaurant in Simsbury is once again called Pettibone Tavern in honor of its first owner, John Pettibone, a very *dis*honorable man responsible for creating Simsbury's most famous ghost: that of his wife, Abigail.

Abigail was caught in the arms of her lover when her husband returned home earlier than expected from a trip. He cut off her head on the spot and chopped her lover to death in her bedroom, Room 6. But decapitating her once for her sin wasn't enough revenge for Pettibone. He then went through the house and cut off her head from every portrait she was in, including one of her sitting on her mother's lap, which is still on display in the front room of the tavern today, although the head, which was found in the basement in 1973, has been carefully glued back on.

Abigail now haunts the tavern, and you would think she'd be an angry and vengeful ghost, but she's harmless for the most part. The website, www.pettibonetavern.com, has an entire page devoted to their ghost story. It tells of closing managers finding the lights suddenly turned back on as they pull out of the parking lot, and opening managers finding furniture rearranged. "One opening manager," it says, "arrived to find one of the oak Hitchcock chairs smashed into pieces in the middle of the dining room. This was more than enough proof of the supernatural activity, because no mortal could have done that to an indestructible Hitchcock chair." She may still linger in her old bedroom, the scene of the murders, which today is the upstairs ladies' bathroom. Many women have reported feeling watched and a distinct chill in the air as they enter the room. They hear unexplained things, such as their names being called when nobody is there. But these incidents are not enough to drive customers away. Quite the contrary. If John Pettibone thought that Abigail could be forgotten simply by cutting off her head so that nobody would ever see her face again, he was dead wrong. Abigail is Simsbury's most famous ghost, and attracts customers from near and far—and the genuinely historic atmosphere and outstanding cuisine certainly don't hurt.

Phantom Plane Crash

According to *UFO Roundup*, a weekly online compilation of UFO-related events and stories, something fishy was going on over Long Island Sound on January 15, 1997, almost six months to the day of the shocking TWA Flight 800 crash in Moriches Bay, some thirty-five miles northeast of the town Westbrook. After a resident of Westbrook spotted a single-engine plane taking a nosedive into the waters of the sound while having his morning coffee, a large-scale rescue effort was immediately put into motion. Even though the man admitted he hadn't seen a splash, one hundred square miles of water was searched. The January 16 edition of *The Day of New London* said the Coast Guard, Department of Environmental Protection, fire departments from four neighboring towns, rescue helicopters, marine patrols, and private citizens all took part in the search. Later that day, when no trace of any aircraft had been found and no airport in the area had received any missing-plane reports, the Coast Guard called off the search. Residents were left baffled by the plane crash apparition.

Phantom plane crashes are a relatively recent phenomenon, but then again, airplanes are a relatively recent creation in the whole scheme of history. Nevertheless, a number of cases have been reported in addition to this incident in Connecticut. Usually a plane is seen taking a nosedive, sometimes by a number of people at once. The explosion of impact may be seen or felt, smoke may be seen, and gasoline may even be smelled. A hasty search is undertaken, which yields no evidence of a plane crash at all: no wreckage, no bodies, no records that any plane was even in the area of impact at the time.

The Long Island Sound incident was typical of this type of phenomenon, but in this case, it wasn't the first time an unidentified flying object was seen over the site of the TWA Flight 800 crash. A month earlier, according to a December 13, 1996, news article titled "Saudi Airlines Pilot Reports 'Flare' Near TWA Site," a "green, flare-like object" was observed by a Saudi Arabian Airlines pilot and detected on radar. It was quickly discounted by the FAA as a meteor. Amazingly, a Pakistani Airlines pilot had made a similar report a month earlier and was told the same thing: a meteor. Imagine the odds of two meteors being spotted in the exact same location one month apart. The likelihood seems greater that it was a paranormal phenomenon, especially given that a phantom plane crash was seen shortly afterward in the same area. This is not unlike the epidemic of green fireballs spotted in New Mexico and the Southwest during a three-year period starting in 1948. Pilots who witnessed the aerial phenomenon all agreed that what they saw were definitely not meteors and most often described the objects as "greenish flares." Witnesses were quickly told by the government that the objects they saw were natural . . . but difficult to explain. How convenient.

The Starr Encounter

On December 16, 1957, Mary Starr had an experience that became one of Connecticut's most famous UFO sightings and encounters.

She was living alone in a cottage on Long Island Sound in Old Saybrook when the bizarre incident occurred. With neighbors few and far between, Starr had nobody to turn to as the events of that night unfolded, and she had nobody who could later corroborate her story. As a Yale graduate with two degrees, however, she was not the type to fabricate such a story. In fact, because of her fine reputation within the community and her academic background, her firsthand account—incredible as it seemed—was accepted as authentic by the UFO research community of that time.

Starr told nobody about her encounter for nearly a year, but when she finally filed a report in 1958, the details of her encounter were still as vivid in her mind as they were the day it occurred. The now-defunct Civilian Saucer Intelligence of NY (CSI) published her account in its July 15, 1959, newsletter after a thorough interview and investigation, saying, "To the growing list of types of 'little men' in UFOs must now be added another, appearing from an unusually reliable source." Starr was so convincing and was such a credible witness that CSI placed her case in the coveted "authentic" category of UFO encounters, hence its rise to fame.

As the CSI report describes it, "On the night of December 15–16, 1957, she was awakened from a sound sleep sometime between 2 and 3 A.M. by bright lights passing her bedroom window which faces north." She then saw a "huge machine 20 or 30 feet long," which was either dark gray or black and had brilliantly lit square portholes. The object hovered motionless about five feet off the ground yet had no wings or external structures to keep it airborne. Through the portholes, she saw two figures with handless arms raised over their heads pass by each other. "They wore a kind of jacket, and she thought they were stewards, carrying trays—except that their heads were unusual. They were square or rectangular, of reddish-orange, with a brighter red 'bulb' in each." She couldn't see their feet, as her view was obscured. The object took a series of unnatural turns and dips, then shot off into the night sky silently. Although others didn't come forward to say they had seen anything that particular night, a few weeks earlier several witnesses had seen unidentified reddish objects that were large in number and brighter than typical stars.

South Central Connecticut

SOUTH CENTRAL CONNECTICUT INCLUDES NINETEEN TOWNS THAT MAKE up the Greater New Haven area. This little region is anchored by the historic city of New Haven and Yale University. It is no surprise that the region abounds in cultural activities. What is surprising is how a region so small can harbor ghost stories so big. The very haunted Charles Island, located off Silver Sands State Beach, has a lot of ghost stories attached to it, including one about "a screeching, flaming skeleton descending from the sky" toward two treasure hunters, who quickly fled the scene. Fort Nathan Hale apparently has a haunted cannon. Midnight Mary haunts the Evergreen Cemetery in New Haven, and her tombstone bears the warning "The people shall be troubled at midnight and pass away." New Haven's Old Union Trust Building is gloriously active with spirits from the past. Sarah Pardee Winchester, of the New Haven Winchester empire, lost everything that mattered to her in Connecticut, and on the advice of a psychic speaking to her on behalf of "the other side," she moved to California, where she built what is dubbed "the most mysterious house ever built." New Haven was also the source of a tale about a phantom ship that returned from the dead just once to say good-bye before vanishing back into the ocean. We shall begin with Albert Bender and the *real* Men in Black.

Albert Bender and the Men in Black

You've probably seen the "Men in Black" movies featuring men sharply dressed in finely tailored black suits and dark glasses, with no-nonsense attitudes, on a mission to save the world from aliens plotting to blow it up. Well, did you know that those movies have their origins in reported incidents involving men dressed in black who apparently are very knowledgeable about extraterrestrial aliens and unidentified flying objects? And for some reason, they attempt to silence people who claim to have seen a UFO or had an encounter with aliens.

One of the earliest reported run-ins with these real-life Men in Black was made known, albeit hesitantly, by Albert K. Bender of Bridgeport, Connecticut, in 1957. An avid flying saucer believer and amateur investigator, Bender founded the International Flying Saucer Bureau (IFSB) and produced a quarterly publication called the *Space Review*. He attempted to contact aliens, if there were any to contact, through experimental group mental telepathy. In his book *Flying Saucers and the Three Men,* Bender described the experiment:

On March 15, 1953, in my den at Bridgeport at exactly 6:00 P.M., I proceeded to take part in the experiment as planned. I put out the lights in my room and then quietly lay down on my bed. After studying the saucers for eleven years, I felt that I would try anything that might help solve the mystery. Saucer investigation had become the biggest part of my life, and I had worked diligently to reach a solution. As soon as I was comfortably situated on the bed, I closed my eyes and began to repeat the message over and over—three times, to be exact.

It was after the third attempt that I felt a terrible, cold chill hit my whole body. Then my head began to ache as if several headaches had saved up their anguish and heaped it upon me at one time. A strange odour reached my nostrils—like that of burning sulphur or badly decomposed eggs. Then I partly lost consciousness as the room around me began to fade away.

Then small blue lights seemed to swim through my brain, and they seemed to blink like the flashing light of an ambulance. I seemed to be floating on a cloud in the middle of space, with a strange feeling of weightlessness controlling my entire anatomy. A throbbing pain developed in my temples and they felt as if they might burst. The parts of my forehead directly over my eyes seemed to be puffed up. I felt cold, very cold, as if I were lying naked on a floating piece of ice in the Antarctic Ocean.

I opened my eyes, and to my amazement I seemed to be floating above my bed but looking down upon it where I imagined I could see my own body lying there! It was as if my soul had left my body and I was hovering above it about three feet in mid-air. Suddenly I could hear a voice which permeated me but in some way did not seem to be an audible sound. The voice seemed to come from the room in front of me, which remained pitch dark.

Bender was then given the following very stern warning via mental telepathy: "We have been watching you and your activities. Please be advised to discontinue delving into the mysteries of the universe. We will make an appearance if you disobey."

The entire incident was very unsettling. He worried whether to divulge this occurrence to his fellow IFSB members or publish the event in the *Space Review*. Discounting both options, he wrote down his account of the night and locked the report in a lockbox at the IFSB office while he contemplated whom to send it to. When he went to retrieve it some days later, it had vanished. Bender admitted that one of the IFSB officers may have removed it, but no one ever confessed to the theft.

Several weeks later, Bender said, he was "visited" by three shadowy figures dressed in black, who strongly urged him to reconsider his plan to report the nighttime incident. They even had a copy of his missing report! This second "conversation" unnerved him so badly that he issued two shocking statements in the October 1953 edition of *Space Review*. The first said: "LATE BULLETIN. A source which the IFSB considers very reliable has informed us that the investigation of the flying saucer mystery and the solution is approaching its final stages."

The second was even more extreme: "STATEMENT OF IMPORTANCE: The mystery of the flying saucers is no longer a mystery. The source is already known, but any information about this is being withheld by order from a higher source. We would like to print the full story in *Space Review*, but because of the nature of the information, we are very sorry that we have been advised in the negative." The statement ended with a clear warning that reverberated throughout the UFO community: "We advice those engaged in saucer work to please be very cautious."

With that, Bender temporarily halted publication of the *Space Review* and disbanded the IFSB. Lem M'Collum stated in the December 1953 edition of *The Saucerian*, "The International Flying Saucer Bureau, a worldwide fact-seeking organization with headquarters at 784 Broad St., Bridgeport, has been ordered, apparently by the government, to cease its activities." Members and subscribers of Bender's *Space Review* insisted on more of an explanation, but Bender did not reply, or replied only cryptically at best.

Albert Bender initially thought that the Men in Black he had encountered were government agents who were sent to quiet him because he had stumbled onto something he was not supposed to know. But his suspicion gave way to apprehension as he gravitated toward believing that they were extraterrestrials.

The Men in Black usually are reported as appearing in groups of three but also have been seen singly, in pairs, and in as many as four in one group. They seem to arrive without warning, just showing up. They are dressed in black suits and shoes with bright white shirts. They usually wear hats. They have no facial hair, including eyebrows. Some have been described as wearing lipstick. Their skin either is well tanned or appears Asian in origin. Their eyes are almond-shaped and glow eerily. Their movements are either very robotic and mechanical or fluid and effortless. In general, their demeanor ranges from ominous to outright threatening. Bender's description of his visitors generally fits this characterization of the Men in Black.

They typically visit witnesses of UFOs or the investigators of the cases rather quickly after the incidents . . . too soon for information about the incidents to have been disseminated broadly. And the men have details that they could not have known without having witnessed the events themselves. They ask numerous, specific questions of the UFO observers and almost always deliver a warning before they leave. Their warnings, which occur in many forms, sternly caution people not to reveal any more information about their sightings or encounters to anyone. Such experiences invariably leave people with feelings of fear and apprehension. The chilling experience of meeting the Men in Black has been described as sinister, menacing, and intimidating. Many people are reluctant to repeat the stories of their UFO sightings or meetings with the Men in Black after such encounters.

From the late 1950s to the present time, there have been hundreds of similar reports of UFO sightings followed by intimidating visits to the observers by odd, dark-suited men who warn against speaking of what was seen. Most of these accounts have originated in the United States, but Britain, Mexico, Sweden, and Italy have also reported Men in Black interactions. Claims of such visits were also reported from Australia and New Zealand in the late 1950s and early 1960s. At least one report arose from mainland China, a nation in which such supernatural discussions are taboo; the witness in that case was a six-year-old boy, hardly an age at which he could have been aware of the phenomenon. Even adult Chinese citizens would not have a cultural reference from which to concoct stories of Men in Black, so that particular case was especially believable— there was no good reason *not* to believe it. The boy, in Yangguan, Shansi province, had an encounter with a UFO in May 1963. The day after he saw the silvery object hanging in the sky, he was stopped by "a very tall man dressed entirely in black" in the street. The man pointed to the exact spot where the boy had seen the disk and asked him if he had seen anything unusual in the sky recently. The child said that he had, and the strange man responded with a warning "never to tell anyone else" what he had seen. In this case, several others saw the Man in Black, reporting his unusual mechanical movements, robotic voice, and unmoving lips even as he spoke.

It may be more plausible that the federal government was involved in the Men in Black visits if they all occurred within the United States. But encounters have been reported in several countries, and it is unlikely that all of their governments have conspired or responded to UFO witnesses in like fashion with stern meetings by men in dark suits. Why would all these people report so similar a pattern from such far reaches of our planet?

Albert Bender put Bridgeport, Connecticut, on the map, not for its well-known history, but for history in the making. *Flying Saucers and the Three Men* can still be found in some used-book stores or through out-of-print booksellers online. Bender was born in 1921, served during World War II with the Air Force, and was a supervisor at the Acme Shear Factory in Bridgeport at the time he formed the IFSB and had his encounters. After the threats he received from the Men in Black and ridicule from the public and press, he dropped out of the UFO business and moved to the West Coast, where he lives an inconspicuous life today.

Charles Island

Located approximately one mile off the shore of Silver Sands State Park at high tide is an island with a rich history of mystery and intrigue, Charles Island. It was part of an area known as Wepawaug by the Paugussett Indians, who referred to the island itself as Poquahaug. Since it was first "sold" by the chief of the Paugussett tribe for ten blankets, some tools, and a dozen mirrors in 1639, no venture or residence has been successfully established on the island. In fact, the island is believed by some to have been cursed, not once but at least three times over the last three hundred years!

The first curse was by an Indian chief whose tribe fought the English settlers for the island, which the Indians believed was sacred—and "spirited"—ground. After the settlers defeated the Indians, the chief proclaimed, "Any shelter will crumble to the Earth, and he shall be cursed," in an attempt to keep the island isolated.

Legend has it that the notorious Captain Kidd buried some of his plunder on the island in 1699, while he was hiding along the Connecticut coastline. Kidd's supposed treasure seems to be buried all along coastal New England! To protect his spoils, Captain Kidd cursed anyone, especially other pirates, who attempted to dig up his buried treasure with certain death.

Another rumor of buried loot on the island originated some twenty-two years later and produced the last of the known curses. As the story goes, five sailors stole a Mexican emperor's treasure from a cave in that country in 1721 and brought it back to Milford, Connecticut. The emperor proclaimed a curse on the stolen treasure. After four of the five sailors suffered a tragic death, the lone survivor transported the booty out to Charles Island, bringing that curse along with him as well.

Many have sought to discover the whereabouts of the legendary treasure chests. Most notably were two treasure seekers who, in 1850, claimed to have uncovered an iron chest buried on the island. As they attempted to lift the encrusted chest from its resting place, they saw a headless figure appear from the sky, surrounded in brilliant

blue flames, and heard a shrill whistling sound. They described it as a "screeching, flaming skeleton descending from the sky." It lurched into the pit where the treasure lay, sending forth a shower of blue flames. The two would-be treasure seekers hastily left the island, dropping their tools right then and there. The following day, after regaining at least some of their composure, and thinking that they must have imagined the impossible spectacle, the pair made their way back out to Charles Island and the site of their discovery. They approached only to find that their tools had vanished and the entire digging site had been covered smoothly with earth and sand, as if it had never been disturbed. Either they truly had imagined the spectacle . . . or there was a supernatural explanation. Whichever the case, the two men allegedly fell victim to the curse and spent the rest of their lives in an insane asylum. At least, that's what some versions of the story say. Others say that the spirits of the Paugussett Indians beheaded the men for digging up their land and made the buried treasure invisible.

According to theshadowlands.net, a massive index of haunted places on the Internet, the curse didn't stop there. At the end of the eighteenth century, a monastery was built on the island by monks who considered the curse silly, calling it "pagan savagery" and "Indian folklore." But a series of unfortunate incidents, including mysterious deaths, suicides, madness, and undeniable hauntings, forced them to leave the island, abandoning the monastery, whose crumbling ruins can still be seen today. Another cocky entrepreneur decided to tempt fate, opening a seaside restaurant and lodge on the island, but a deadly fire caused by an unknown source destroyed the restaurant. Nobody has attempted to build on the island since then, but many people still visit there, often returning with stories of glowing ghosts in the trees and the sounds of disembodied voices and music and festivities from the past. Some even claim that a few phantom monks continue to make their processionals through the monastery ruins.

Most recently, a proposal to construct a gas pipeline in 2002 included one alternative that routed the pipeline under the sediments in the water around the west and south portions of Charles Island. This alternative was rejected because of the difficulties of accurately boring two long, horizontal pipeline segments. Or could it be that someone learned of the long line of unsuccessful enterprises that had started and failed on Charles Island?

Charles Island is connected to the mainland during low tides by a sandbar. The mystique of the island's history has tempted beachgoers to walk out to the island, but the entire island is now a nature preserve, and a fence encircles the island, posted with a No Trespassing sign. The temporary island causeway has several hazards including slippery rocks and strong tidal currents. One misstep while the tide is coming in, and curious explorers may find themselves being carried away from the sandbar by the strong currents, which is probably why the island is posted. Landing of watercraft on the beaches is also prohibited, and the island is patrolled.

Fort Nathan Hale

In early 1776, the colony of Connecticut commissioned the construction of a fort on a point of rock that stretched out into the harbor to protect the port of New Haven from the British. This was the location of an earlier unnamed fort from circa 1657, and on this site was erected Black Rock Fort. Unfortunately for the colonists, in 1779 in the Battle of New Haven, the British captured Black Rock Fort along with its nineteen defenders, but only after they had run out of ammunition! The British burned the wooden barracks as they left. In 1807, the abandoned fort was reconstructed as Fort Nathan Hale, and it served to defend the port from the British again during the War of 1812. In 1863, Fort Nathan Hale II was built alongside the original fort, out of concern that Southern raiders might strike the city during the Civil War, but the fort saw no battle action. This fort contained deep, earthen, bomb-proof bunkers.

Much of the fort now has been restored, including the bunkers, moat, drawbridge, and fortifications. Add to the authentic restoration efforts a few phantom soldiers in the mix, and you'll feel as if you truly are back in time. People have reported sightings of ghostly soldiers and glowing green orbs in the bunkers of the fort. Some accounts attribute the soldier apparitions to a battle that took place at the fort, but the bunkers were constructed as part of Fort Nathan Hale II, which never saw battle. Whether the energy from the earlier forts still permeates the current structure is the question.

Also of interest at Fort Nathan Hale is a cannon that was donated to the fort sometime after the 1950s. Not much is known of this cannon other than the recounted memories of two gentlemen who were present when it was donated, but it is believed to have come from the privateer sloop *Mars,* which sailed out of Guilford Harbor and Long Island Sound. The *Mars* was initially an American vessel but supposedly was captured by the British in 1778, only to be retaken by the colonists of Guilford later in the Revolutionary War. Another possibility for the presence of the orbs is that the cannon may be haunted by its previous users or crewmembers of the ship that it was retrieved from. It seems that spirit energy is often attached to specific objects rather than to individuals or locations, especially if the object held some life-altering importance to the person who used it before he or she died. Though there are no records of anyone having died on the *Mars,* that's not to say it didn't happen. Lack of records was not uncommon in those days.

The fort is listed on the National Register of Historic Places and is currently operated by the City of New Haven. It is open daily to the public for tours and interpretation. However, interpretation of the glowing orbs and figures that have been seen and described is up to you.

Midnight Mary

anabiosis (AN-uh-bye-OH-sis): restoration to life from a deathlike state

Possibly one of the most well-recounted tales in the New Haven area, and in all of Connecticut, is of the apparent death and burial—or burial, *then* death—of Mary E. Hart, better known as Midnight Mary.

Born in New Haven in 1824, Mary Hart was an unassuming woman who worked as a machine stitcher and corset maker and lived somewhere in the Winthrop Avenue area. Around noon on October 15, 1872, at the age of forty-seven, Mary abruptly fell into a deathlike state from unknown causes. By midnight, the grieving family, believing that their Mary had indeed died, arranged to have her body interred immediately. The night following her burial, Mary's beloved aunt had a horribly vivid nightmare in which she saw Mary struggling inside her coffin, scratching at the lining to get out, and moaning horrifically. It caused the aunt such anxiety that the family ordered the coffin in Evergreen Cemetery exhumed. They removed the lid to discover a heart-stopping sight: Mary's body lay in a contorted position, her hands injured, fingertips ripped off, and fingers twisted. The lining of the coffin had been torn to pieces by the woman, who had obviously tried to claw her way out!

The cause of Mary Hart's deathlike appearance that led her family to hastily bury her is not known, but it was generally believed in those days to have been a massive stroke or apoplexy. Other real possibilities of that time period include lead poisoning, algae- or parasite-delivered neurotoxins, or even a temporary lack of oxygen to her brain, all of which could have caused her to appear dead. At the time that Mary lived, it was tradition that the deceased person's body would be laid out and attended to until it was removed for burial, typically three days. But in this case, under the family's orders, burial was almost immediate—a fact that undoubtedly haunted them the rest of their lives, for if they had waited the customary amount of time, she would have awakened on the second day, since her body had not been embalmed. Embalming was a relatively new procedure, not widely offered or accepted at that time, and one that ensured no chance of survival.

Consumed by guilt, the family erected the huge pink granite marker over Mary's grave with the following well-known inscription in large, bold, black letters, curved across the top of the tombstone: THE PEOPLE SHALL BE TROUBLED AT MIDNIGHT AND PASS AWAY. Smaller letters below that foreboding statement read: AT HIGH NOON JUST FROM AND ABOUT TO RENEW HER DAILY WORK, IN HER FULL STRENGTH OF BODY AND MIND MARY E. HART, HAVING FALLEN PROSTRATE, REMAINED UNCONCIOUS, UNTIL SHE DIED AT MIDNIGHT, OCTOBER 15, 1872. BORN DECEMBER 16, 1824. No one can confirm whether the family actually designed that stone or thought up its unusual inscription. And no one knows for certain what the larger words meant, then or now. Some have speculated that the family felt Mary deserved to be known and famous, because she had lived such a humble and isolated life, so they came up with an inscription sure to make all who read it remember her name.

Another story of Miss Hart's demise implies that she was actually a witch, and that the inscription on her headstone is a continuing warning to all who would consider disturbing her grave. This tale doesn't end with her passing, though. Legends abound of persons entering the graveyard at night and staying until midnight, when Mary's spirit—if she were truly a witch—supposedly inflicts the consequences on those who violate her grave. Teenagers, college students, and sailors all are said to have stayed too long at the grave past midnight, only to have injury or death befall them. One teenager was killed in a traffic accident the day after his overnight visit to Mary's grave. Three sailors were reported to have been impaled when they tried to climb out over the iron-spire fencing that completely surrounds the cemetery after being scared away by something or someone. Another young man's body was found in the cemetery the day after he and a companion attempted to remain at her grave. His pant leg was held fast by a thorn bush, and his face displayed agonized fear. These all are urban legends that are prolifically retold but cannot be either confirmed or rebutted.

Other stories say that some who inadvertently have passed by Mary's grave have been afflicted by the woman's curse. A horse and wagon once passing by the main gate of the cemetery at precisely the stroke of midnight simply sank from witnesses' view, as if it were being swallowed by quicksand, they said. And Cinderella thought she had it bad at the stroke of midnight! Then there was a young man who picked up a hitchhiker on Davenport Avenue and dropped her off, as she requested, at a house that sits directly across the road from Mary's gravestone on Winthrop Avenue. The next day, he stopped by the house to make sure the ragged-looking woman who introduced herself simply as Mary was doing better. Imagine his surprise when the elderly man who answered the door told him nobody by that name lived there.

The Old Union Trust Building

One cannot help but notice the unusual shape of the Union Trust building, which fills up the entire corner of Elm Street and Church Street in downtown New Haven with its thirteen stories. But its shape is not the only thing unusual about this structure. According to a website called "The Haunted Skyscraper," shadowy images of people, sounds of hands slapping against walls, footfalls, toilets flushing, lights turning on and off, loud banging noises, and voices of people talking when no one was in the building have been reported a remarkable sixty-eight times (at least!) since the late 1990s. People working alone in the building when it was closed have clearly heard their names being called. The phenomena have been experienced by numerous unrelated people and occur at all times of the day or night on many of the building's thirteen floors and in the basement.

The basement is particularly active—or unnerving, depending on your point of view. It contains the boiler room, an unused café, restrooms, and numerous other spaces connected by a series of hallways called "the Maze." Particularly distressing is the sound that has been heard of three palm slaps against the basement walls. No less than four people have heard the distinct sound of an open hand striking the wall of the basement hard and always three times in rapid succession. Massive banging noises and voices that range from clearly spoken words to sorrowful moans have filled the stale basement air, sending the individuals hearing them retreating back up to the lobby.

Figures that have appeared and vanished include tall, thin, dark caricatures, gentlemen in suits, and small, old dwarfs. Many reports of the encounters in and around the Old Union Trust building, as well as photographs, are cataloged thoroughly on "The Haunted Skyscraper." And apparently, not only is the interior of the Union Trust building a source of paranormal activity, but the surrounding area is as well. A dark, unidentified figure of a person has been seen numerous times in all sorts of weather conditions, always just before dawn, moving past the front lawn of the building. Perhaps it's a visiting ghost from the massive New Haven Green burial ground directly across the street. It's believed to hold ten thousand bodies interred there from 1638 to 1821. When the headstones were moved to the Grove Street Cemetery, the actual bodies were left behind, still buried in the green.

The Emerson apartment building, just behind the Union Trust building, also claims a wealth of unusual events. David Pitkin describes the apartment building as one of the most haunted places in New Haven in *Ghosts of the Northeast*. Shortly after an elderly man died in his apartment in this building, he was seen walking by a local diner and peering in by waitresses. Some old habits *are* hard to break!

Sarah Pardee Winchester

This story crosses the United States from the Atlantic to the Pacific and back again, but it all began in New Haven. Born in September 1839 in New Haven, Sarah Lockwood Pardee grew up to be a petite and lovely young woman. Standing a mere four feet, ten inches, she was said to have had a wonderful disposition, a charismatic personality, and a talent for speaking several languages fluently. Sarah married William Wirt Winchester, the only son of the extremely successful entrepreneur and businessman Oliver Fisher Winchester of New Haven, on September 30, 1862. With that, Sarah Winchester became the "belle of New Haven" and moved into the Winchester Mansion at 194 Prospect. The house is no longer there, but the wrought-iron fence at the bottom of the hill on St. Ronan Street still marks the property.

The elder Mr. Winchester earned the first part of his fortune in the shirt-making industry and in 1850 invested in the Volcanic Repeating Arms Company, which would later bear his name as the Winchester Repeating Arms Company. William Winchester took over the gun-manufacturing company in 1857, allowing his father to enjoy a career in politics as lieutenant governor of Connecticut and philanthropy. With the development of several famous improvements to the repeating rifle, sales of guns to the government and private individuals exploded, and by the 1880s, the company had more than six hundred employees. The family's fortune increased consistently . . . but misfortune was just around the corner.

Sarah Pardee Winchester had a daughter, Annie, in 1866. Shortly thereafter, tragedy struck. Less than one month old, little Annie Winchester died of an illness called marasmus, also known as malnutrition or wasting away. It is usually caused by protein or calorie deficiency but can have other causes. Sarah became so deeply depressed at the loss of her only child that she withdrew from society—and her husband—and was said to have been on the edge of madness for almost ten years. Not long after she finally returned to the New Haven mansion, tragedy struck again. In 1880, Oliver Winchester passed away, and the Winchester fortune became William's. But he was only to enjoy it for a very short time. In March 1881, William Wirt Winchester died of tuberculosis at the age of forty-three, leaving almost 50 percent of the Winchester fortune to his widow, Sarah. At that time, her portion of the company was estimated to be valued at $20 million, and in those days, it was not taxed.

But Sarah would not be consoled by such an inheritance. All of the people she had loved were dead. She was so grief-stricken that she consulted a medium, possibly named Adam Coons (it has been debated whether Mrs. Winchester sought a male or female medium), to attempt to contact her dead husband. However, the message she received did not come from William Winchester, but was instead a warning from the spirits of the many people who had been killed by Winchester rifles, seeking vengeance for the innumerable deaths: "There is a curse on your life. It is the same curse that took your child and husband that has resulted from the terrible weapon that the Winchester family created. . . . [B]uild a house not only for yourself but also for the spirits of those who have fallen before that terrible weapon. As long as you build, you will live. Stop and you will die," was what one seer allegedly told her, according to Joe Nickel of the online *Skeptical Inquirer.*

Incidentally, the deadliness of the Winchester arms can be seen in the account of an attempted bank robbery in Deep River, Connecticut, in 1899. The Deep River National Bank had received a warning that it would be the target of another bank robbery after "the moon has waned and the nights grow darker." The bank had been the subject of several previous, unsuccessful robbery plots. Harry Tyler, the bank's watchman, obtained a Winchester gun that had the reputation of being capable of killing two men with a single blast. On that fateful night of December 13, the guard observed four men approaching the rear of the bank and attempting to pry open one of the bank's windows. One of the four had in his possession a revolver. The guard aimed and fired his weapon, dropping one of the suspects. The three others scattered and were never found. Upon examination of the killed burglar, it was discovered that the Winchester had blown away a fair portion of the left side of his face.

Sarah believed that the "terrible weapon," as the psychic put it, the very instrument of her family fortune, had truly cursed her with loss of life, as she'd been told. As long as she was connected to that money, she would never find peace. After her husband's death, William Converse, who was married to Sarah's sister, became president of Winchester Repeating Arms Company. So Sarah's family continued to operate the gun-manufacturing company, maintaining her association with the cursed money.

Nevertheless, as directed by the warning, to appease the spirits, Sarah sold her house in New Haven and moved west in search of a location that she would "recognize" to purchase and begin a new life. Guided by what she believed was the invisible hand of her late husband, Sarah bought a doctor's house that was under construction in California's Santa Clara Valley in 1884. She hired servants, carpenters, plumbers, and masons and continually built on and added to the structure. Apparently, the number thirteen was of special significance to Sarah in the building process, since—superstitious as she was—she had a great respect for its reputed powers. Many of the stairs had thirteen steps, many windows had thirteen panes, and many walls consisted of thirteen panels.

Stories quickly spread about strange occurrences taking place at the sprawling mansion, including séances, disembodied voices, and fleeting shadows. These continued throughout Sarah's lifetime and were purported to be encouraged by her, as a result of her attempts to appease the angry spirits. Once residing on the property where she intended to create her unending mansion, she became even more reclusive, seeing only a very few relatives or visitors. A single photograph of her exists from the period of 1884 to 1922.

Sarah Pardee Winchester died in 1922 in the house she built and expanded on for thirty-eight years. When the safe from her mansion was opened, valuables of a sentimental type, rather than the anticipated monetary treasures, were discovered: locks of hair from her husband and baby, along with their obituaries. Sarah's will was thirteen pages long, and she had signed it thirteen times. Her body was transported back to New Haven, Connecticut, where she was interred alongside her husband and infant daughter. A large, rough-hewn granite rock with the Winchester name marks the three graves at the Evergreen Cemetery.

The famed escape artist Harry Houdini visited the Winchester mansion and even attended a midnight séance, but not until 1924, two years after Mrs. Winchester's death. The phenomena experienced at the Winchester Mansion while it was being constructed have not ceased with the passing of Sarah Winchester. It is reported that voices, orbs, strange sounds, and cold spots continue to plague this now famous tourist attraction and national historic site. If these are the voices and communiqués of those same spirits that cursed the Winchester family, they may still be seeking vengeance, especially since the very weapons that Sarah Pardee Winchester sought to release herself from are now on display for tourists to see in a museum at her mansion!

The Storm Ship

From Charles Skinner's *Myths and Legends of Our Own Land: Tales of a Puritan Land* comes another gem I'd be remiss in not passing along.

In 1647, the New Haven colonists, who even at that early day exhibited the enterprise that has been a distinguishing feature of the Yankee, sent a ship to Ireland to try to develop a commerce, their trading posts on the Delaware having been broken up by the Swedes. When their agent, Captain Lamberton, sailed in January, the harbor was so beset with ice that a track had to be cut through the floes to open water, five miles distant. She had, moreover, to be dragged out stern foremost—an ill omen, the sailors thought—and as she swung before the wind, a passing drift of fog concealed her for a moment from the gaze of those on shore, who, from this, foretold things of evil.

In those days, as perhaps today, there were thought to be many omens of ill fortune to be noted for ships setting out to sea. In this case, the ship being dragged out to open water stern-first and the transient fog that momentarily occluded the ship from view, may have foretold her impending disappearance. It probably didn't help when a clergyman on shore offered the grim, albeit well-meaning, prayer: "Lord, if it be thy pleasure to bury these, our friends, in the bottom of the sea, take them. They are thine. Save them."

According to Skinner, those words were soon taken literally. The ship was only seen one more time, the following year—a mere shadow of its former self, a phantom ship.

Winter passed. So did spring. Still the ship came not; but one afternoon in June, just as a rain had passed, some children cried, "There's a brave ship!," for flying up the harbor with all sail set and flaunting colors was a vessel, "the very mould of our ship," the clergyman said.

Strange to tell, she was going flat against the wind. No sailors were on her deck; she did not toss with the fling of the waves. There was no ripple at her bow. As she came close to land, a single figure appeared on the quarter, pointing seaward with a cutlass. Then suddenly her main top fell, her masts toppled from their holdings, and the dismantled hulk careened and went down. A cloud dropped from Heaven and brooded for a time above the place where it had vanished, and when it lifted, the surface of the sea was empty and still. The good folk of New Haven believed that the fate of the absent ship had been revealed, at last, for she never came back and Captain Lamberton was never heard from.

Eastern Connecticut

EASTERN CONNECTICUT IS KNOWN AS MYSTIC COUNTRY, AND THE NORTH- eastern region is often called the Quiet Corner, where vacationers, especially from New York City, return year after year to relax and get away from it all. That's not to say Mystic Country is boring by any means. It is home to the world's largest casino, Foxwoods in Ledyard, and the Mystic Seaport, one of New England's most visited attractions. But there is much more to Eastern Connecticut than antique shops, seaports, casinos, and seafood restaurants. There are (or were) vampires; lost villages (but we found 'em!); haunted homesteads, lighthouses, restaurants, and inns; frogs gone mad, and the ensuing frog worshipers; and one of the greatest psychic mediums who ever lived.

In Mystic Country, you'll find the Nathan Hale Homestead in South Coventry, said to be haunted by Hale family members and servants; Captain Grant's inn, haunted by the captain's wife and sons; the Homespun Farm in Griswold, where Old Man Simon offers his opinion from beyond the grave; and the John York House in North Stonington, where two men who were best friends died in a battle over a lady. The enigmatic D. D. Home, psychic extraordinaire, spent some time in Eastern Connecticut perfecting his many unnatural talents. Gungywamp in the town of Groton sounds like the name of a B movie, but it's actually the site of many mysterious rock formations, including stone piles called cairns, stone circles, standing pillar stones, and stone chambers with mysterious powers. The Ledge Light in New London is a lighthouse haunted by the ghost of Ernie, the lighthouse keeper, and the nearby Lighthouse Inn is haunted by a bride who tumbled down the circular staircase and died on her wedding day. North Stonington has Randall's Ordinary Landmark Inn, which is haunted by a sad, older gentleman carrying an early gun, and Mystic has the Red Brook Inn, which is haunted by two women. One watches over and protects the guests when they forget to open their fireplace flues, and the other seeks revenge on a woman she banned from the house who kept coming back. Griswold is home to the famous so-called Jewett City vampires, which were buried—and then unearthed—there.

I find it rather ironic and humorous that of the three stories from the Quiet Corner, two are specifically about noise! Bara-Hack near Pomfret is called, among other things, "the Village of Voices," because the day-to-day sounds of a thriving little community from yesteryear have been heard by many who visit the abandoned site deep in the woods, far from any actual inhabitants. It's as if today's people are somehow able to eavesdrop on a past civilization that isn't even aware of our presence but is clearly alive and thriving in "their" time. Perhaps they hear and see fleeting glimpses of us through that same thin, interdimensional "veil," making them wonder if *we're* ghosts or something unexplainable from another time.

The other noisy story perhaps should have been called "The Night of the Living (then Dead) Frogs," for it was truly a nightmare at the time for the residents of Windham. It happened in 1754, but it made the town so instantly famous (and the butt of many jokes from other towns that must have needed a good laugh in those days) that the mysterious incident involving thousands of frogs is celebrated to this day. You'll find froggy images all over Windham, even on its official village seal.

Apples seem to connote everything good: wholesome, all-American, one a day keeps the doctor away. . . . But the story from Franklin, also in the northeastern region, will have you thinking differently about apples the next time you bite into one. It offers an explanation for the origination of the Micah Rood apple, which should have been called the Blood Apple, as well as the Rood Tree. And they call it the Quiet Corner!

The Amazing D. D. Home

Daniel Douglas (D. D.) Home was one of the greatest psychic mediums of all time, and he developed his incredible abilities right here in Eastern Connecticut. Born in Edinburgh, Scotland, in 1833, Home (pronounced Hume) moved to America to be raised by his aunt when he was just nine. But he was quite the handful, with his strange powers and overall poor health due to tuberculosis, and his aunt had all she could do to raise the unusual child for the seven years that she did. Eventually, D. D.'s talk of being constantly surrounded by spirits became too much for the woman to bear, and she turned him out on the streets, fearing that his unusual behavior was the work of the devil. So at fifteen years old, D.D. became a "professional houseguest," often performing séances and other feats in exchange for lodging, if only for a day or two.

The difference between Home and other mediums of that time period was that Home was determined to prove he wasn't a fraud, as he believed many of the mediums he had witnessed were. He held his séances in brightly lit rooms and asked that people hold his hands and feet during sessions to prove he wasn't manipulating any objects. Amazingly, his séances produced rappings similar to New York State's Fox sisters' claim to fame. More incredibly, and more difficult to debunk, were ghostly truncated hands that seemed to reach out of midair to shake hands with astonished witnesses. Ghost lights often appeared, objects such as tables and chairs moved unassisted, and phantom music played. Home often explained that he had no idea how or why these things happened in his presence and at his beckoning, but he believed it was the work of good spirits that were always with him. He didn't believe the power came from within himself, but that the feats were performed for his benefit. And then it happened . . .

When he was just nineteen years old, Home's usual stunts suddenly paled before a newfound ability—levitation. It first happened at the home of Connecticut businessman Ward Cheney in full view of Cheney and a newspaper reporter named F. L. Burr, who was visiting the house to write an article that was supposed to prove Home was a fraud. Instead, Home gave him something to *really* talk about, and the reporter quickly became a staunch supporter of the young psychic's abilities. He described what he observed in the

Hartford Times in 1852: "Suddenly, without any expectation of the part of the company, Home was taken up into the air. I had hold of his hand at the time, and I felt his feet—they were lifted a foot from the floor. He palpitated from head to foot with the contending emotions of joy and fear which choked his utterances. Again and again, he was taken from the floor, and the third time, he was taken to the ceiling of the apartment, with which his hands and feet came into gentle contact." The reporter was sure it had not been trickery, as there were no mirrors or ropes in the room.

At age twenty-one, Home moved back to Europe, where he soon became acquainted with many famous and royal individuals, such as Napoleon III, for whom he was more than happy to perform. At twenty-five, he met and married a Russian nobleman's daughter, but she died just four years later after giving birth to their son, Gregoire. In 1868, his most famous levitation of all occurred before a live audience at the home of Lord Adare. After drifting into a trance, Home was said to have floated out the window of a third-floor room and back into another window. Three of the witnesses were beyond reproach: Lord Adaire, Captain Charles Wynne, and the master of Lindsay, all members of London's elite.

Home married again in 1871 and retired from public performances two years later. He died in 1886 at the age of fifty-three, after many years of battling tuberculosis. Though many skeptics, including the famous magician Houdini and other spiritualists and mediums of the time, claimed they could imitate Home's so-called tricks, nobody actually ever did. In his entire career, Home was never caught cheating or proven to be a fraud. He will forever be remembered for his levitation and ability to fly with a little help from his spirit friends.

Bara-Hack

Bara-Hack. The name has a peculiar, paranormal-ish ring to it, doesn't it? While the actual Welsh meaning of the phrase, "breaking of bread," is rather bland, the settlement located off Route 97 near Pomfret is anything but. Bara-Hack is also called the "Lost Village of Pomfret," "Village of Voices," and "Village of Ghostly Voices." But it may not be ghosts, per se, whose voices are heard.

Obadiah Higginbotham and Jonathan Randall settled and named Bara-Hack in 1790, but by the late 1800s, the village was uninhabited. Besides the adequate No Trespassing signs that dot the now-private property, all that remains of Bara-Hack today are a few stone foundations and cellar holes; a small cemetery where generations of Higginbothams, Randalls, and their slaves were laid to rest; and the woods, as deep and dark as they were when Obadiah and Jon first came upon the site. Just outside the cemetery bounds, the great elm in which a phantom infant has been spotted lying since at least the early 1800s still stands, baby and all. A number of individuals have seen the diminutive apparition, both on film and in person. Even in the days before any member of their own community had died, the earliest settlers experienced otherworldly phenomena. For example, the Randalls' slaves saw ghosts, including the baby, in the trees. In the years since, many visitors to the site have said they heard disembodied voices. As well, there have been frequent reports of the sounds of cows mooing, dogs barking, children laughing, and horse-drawn buggies traveling on a road no longer there . . . sounds of a typical village on a typical day, even though it is a mile away from the nearest home.

Odell Shepard, author of *The Harvest of a Quiet Eye*, echoed the growing sentiments about the mystical place when he wrote in 1927: "Although there is no human habitation for a long distance . . . there is always a hum and stir of human life. . . . They hear the laughter of children at play . . . the voices of mothers who have long been dust calling their children . . . the rumble of heavy wagons along an obliterated road. It is as though sounds were able in this place to get round that incomprehensible corner, to pierce that mysterious soundproof wall that we call Time."

Paul Eno wrote of his experiences at Bara-Hack for *FATE* magazine, among others, and in his book *Faces at the Window*. Eno led a famous expedition to the site with a group of college students in 1971. He originally believed the land was simply haunted by earthbound spirits, because the group heard the voices and sounds so often reported and saw several apparitions themselves. "For more than seven minutes we watched a bearded face suspended in the air over the cemetery's western wall, while in an elm tree over the northern wall, we clearly saw a baby-like figure reclining." Today his opinion is more closely aligned with Shepard's, according to "The Bara-Hack Investigation Web Site," and he now believes that perhaps the sounds frequently heard in Bara-Hack are somehow "slipping" through the space-time continuum from another dimension—a matter of quantum physics, he says—whereby people are very much alive in *their* time, yet dead in ours. And they are completely unaware that we are eavesdropping on their daily goings-on . . . or are they?

Captain Grant's, 1754

"Let it be known that on this date, I, William Grant, hath built a home suitable for my wife Mercy and our sons whom God wilth provide for us. God save the King." —February 13, 1754

Captain Grant's, 1754, now an inn located at 109–111 Route 2A in Poquetanuck, was built by Captain William Gonzales Grant in the year of its name for his young wife, Mercy Adelaide Avery, their two sons, a daughter, and himself. But shortly after those proud words were uttered, Captain Grant died at sea at just thirty-two years of age. His heartbroken wife, pregnant with their third son (Captain Grant the Second), continued to live at the house he had built for her, raising her children alone. She passed away in her eighties, but many believe she and perhaps her children continue to roam through the house, now a bed-and-breakfast, in spirit. Owner Carol Matsumo said, "Captains Grant the First and Second are buried with mercy in St. James Cemetery across the road from the house. Captain Grant the Second's tombstone has disappeared for the second time."

In the room called the Adelaide Room, attention-getting incidents occur with enough frequency to make you wonder if it might indeed be haunted. The shower curtain falls inexplicably, and the TV turns on and off on its own. Carol says that many guests have captured orbs on film, and she has photographed an "actual electrical outline" of a ghost. Visitors have reported loud knocking on the doors of Captain Grant's inn, yet when they answer, nobody is there. Carol said, "At the same time on periodic days, a man walks through the attic above the Adelaide room. The timing changes with Daylight Savings Time. It is very loud and wakes up guests. It was this occurrence that made us come clean about our ghosts. We had a New York City detective stay in the Adelaide room. He came downstairs at 7:30 A.M. to confront us about disturbing our guests by walking in the attic above him at 5:00 A.M. We told him that we had a ghost and would prove it to him after breakfast. At that time the attic was used to store lumber for renovations, and the floor above the Adelaide room was completely covered. It would have been impossible for anyone to walk above the room. He has stayed with us three times since." Any number of people could be responsible for haunting the historic inn, which was used as a garrison to house soldiers during the Revolutionary War and as part of the Underground Railroad during the Civil War. Many people have passed through its doors—some who lived out their entire lifetime contentedly in its confines, and others who passed through transiently while under tremendous stress. Many emotions, both good and bad, have left an impression in the atmosphere of the inn, and that's a key ingredient in haunted places everywhere.

Captain Grant's spirit would be pleased to know that in 1996, the home he built and put his heart and soul into was listed on the National Register of Historic Places. Equally pleasing is the fact that the inn was restored to its original splendor that same year, just as Grant had left it. Carol and husband Ted began renovations in 1994, and the authentic restoration coupled with their obvious innkeeping talents made the inn quickly popular. It was featured on Home and Garden TV in January 2002 and recommended by *Maxim* magazine as "a romantic place to take a loved one." *USA Today* listed the bed-and-breakfast as one of the best inns to visit in 2003, and MSNBC.com said it was one of the best places to stay in New England. All of those honors are without the ghost stories, which also make Captain Grant's such a popular destination. In 2003, CNN Headline News featured a story about the inn's annual Halloween Special, which consists of one or more nights in the haunted inn, with ghost stories shared by the innkeepers, as well as a tour of the nearby abandoned Cemetery #17, which Carol says is "probably the spookiest cemetery you would ever want to visit." Guests are encouraged to bring cameras to see if they capture any spirit essence on film. Carol relates that a guest took a picture on one of the tours, "and when the picture was developed, there was a man laying under the leaves. His face was very prominent. Believe me, there was no man actually laying there." The most haunted room to book for the occasion is the Adelaide Room, so make your reservation early.

Gungywamp

No, it's not a monster of the big screen. Gungywamp is one of Connecticut's most outstanding lithic locales, a one hundred-acre site of stone marvels located in Groton. Its unusual name is as mysterious as the various rock formations it contains, for not much is known about the origin of either. The site consists of stone piles, circles, and chambers, as well as rows of standing stone configurations—all evidential of early human settlement. The question is, how early? And by whom? Charcoal found near the stone circles has been dated to several hundred years A.D. Evidence of frequent fire-burning on the large slabs of quarried stone that make up two stone circles has led many to speculate that the circles were used as an ancient altar. Other artifacts discovered there include Colonial-era items. It appears to be an area inhabited by various colonies at various times in history.

On the eastern boundary of Gungywamp are two rows of short, evenly spaced boulders facing in a northerly direction. These have caused much speculation. They were once believed to be the primitive skirting of an animal keep, but the stones are spaced too far apart to have held anything but enormous prehistoric animals. Perhaps more plausible is the theory that these are the remains of a Colonial rock wall, the boulders having acted as the support stones for a structure that no longer stands. No artifacts whatsoever have been dug up near the rows of stones to help date the arrangement, so there's really no certainty as to their origin.

Gungywamp's stone piles, known as rock cairns, are a mystery as well. Rock cairns dot the New England landscape and are often associated with early Colonial land clearing, Indian sites, or ancient quarrying, but there may be more to Gungywamp's cairns than meets the eye. Why else would the rock ledge near the stone piles be called "Cliff of Tears"? People hiking past the site have reported being overcome by feelings of despair to the point that many begin to cry. Others have suffered nosebleeds and bleeding gums while in the area, according to the website "Connecticut: Mysterious New England," which deals with lithics throughout New England. It states that widely fluctuating magnetic fields known to occur in that spot may cause a physical reaction in some people and suggests perhaps that's why there aren't as many artifacts as one might expect to find at Gungywamp—the magnetic fields caused people to feel unwell, so the site was possibly used only for ceremonies of some sort, rather than prolonged occupancy.

Besides the obvious archaeological interest in such an area, a fair amount of paranormal interest has also been generated over the years, not necessarily because anything paranormal is happening there. But the various stone formations are splendidly mystifying and unexplained as yet, which adds to the allure and interest of such a place. The Gungywamp Society, a nonprofit organization made up of volunteers who research and attempt to preserve the land, denies any evidence of Celtic or Viking occupation of the site. Further, it states emphatically that no Bronze Age artifacts have ever been found in the area, only "paleo Indian, Colonial and post-Colonial" relics. And as far as any mysterious energies or powers emanating from any natural structure on the grounds, the group does not encourage paranormal or spiritual interpretations.

That said, Carol Hallas, current board member, librarian, and researcher for the society, did admit in the March 27, 2003, *Hartford Advocate* that the stone formations and structures at Gungywamp are extraordinary. "I've spent a lot of time out in the field," she said, "and I've seen a lot of old stuff. And I've never seen anything like it. And I see a lot of oddball things." She may be referring especially to the four stone chambers. The Calendar Chamber is perhaps the most perplexing, as well as the most functional. It has an opening facing east, which, only during the spring and fall equinoxes, allows the sunlight to penetrate through the larger chamber and directly into the entrance of a small, beehive-shaped internal chamber. The lone ray of light then reflects off a pale wall of stone with heavy garnet concentrations, which illuminates the interior of the smaller chamber twice a year. In this way, the configuration of stones acts as a reliable calendar, just like similar structures in sixth- and seventh-century Ireland, hence the theory that Culdee Monks may have erected the site after fleeing from Ireland.

Another theory for the origin of the chambers suggests that they served as root cellars in early Colonial days, which might explain the Calendar Chamber's ability to predict planting and harvest times. Both the Mohegan and Pequot tribes would like to lay claim to Native American relics that have been unearthed at Gungywamp and have been dated to about four thousand years ago. Each tribe believes its ancestors built the chambers. The truth is, nobody knows for certain who built them, or any other structure on the grounds, but the Gungywamp Society is determined to continue pressing for thorough and ongoing studies of the site by historians and archaeologists until some of those questions can finally be answered.

Hale Homestead

"I only regret that I have but one life to lose for my country." At the time Nathan Hale, Connecticut's official state hero, uttered those final words to his British executioners at their headquarters in Manhattan in September 1776, just as they were about to hang him for spying, he was an unheard-of patriot who had happened to accept a daring mission from the militia. New York City was a spy center during the Revolutionary War, and Hale was just one of hundreds of young spies or scouts fighting for liberty. After his hanging, the body remained in public view for three days, as was customary, before being cut down and callously tossed into an unmarked grave, which has never been found. That's enough to make any soul unable to rest in peace, but Hale accepted his destiny with dignity and courage. He has no reason to haunt his former abode—he holds no gripes and had just the one regret so often repeated over the centuries. Someone may haunt Hale's homestead, but it isn't Nathan Hale.

The Hale family home, at 2299 South Street in Coventry, was built in 1746 when Nathan's father, Deacon Richard Hale, married Elizabeth Strong. The rooms of the original mansion quickly filled to capacity as the Hales' brood grew. Nathan was their sixth child, born in 1755. Elizabeth died at home shortly after the birth—and death—of their twelfth child, leaving Deacon to raise the remaining eleven children alone. Two years later, he met and married a wealthy widow named Abigail Adams, who had seven children of her own. With the expanded family and anticipated grandchildren, it became obvious that an even larger mansion was needed. So Nathan Hale's birthplace was rebuilt and turned into the massive two-family mansion that stands today as the Hale Homestead museum, owned by the Antiquarian and Landmarks Society. Over the course of several decades, a number of members of the large Hale family passed away at the home, and some of them are believed to still haunt it.

When George Dudley Seymour, a huge Nathan Hale fan, purchased the house along with its substantial acreage in 1914, it had lain vacant for years and was in dire need of repair—a task the patent attorney and antiquarian would relish. His mission in life was to restore the dilapidated structure to its original glory, filling it with Hale family artifacts and antiques. He also kept careful notes on ghost stories and legends regarding the Hale Homestead, including his own otherworldly experiences there. Once he had the homestead satisfactorily refurbished, he opened his pride and joy to the public. Upon his death in 1945, it was bequeathed to the Antiquarian and Landmarks Society, which he cofounded. Today the society opens it as a seasonal museum that brings history to life, with employees dressed as members of the Hale family, house tours, and demonstrations of eighteenth- and nineteenth-century ways of life. However, the servant lady you see working in the kitchen or sweeping the upper hall in the early morning may not be an employee playing the part . . . it may be the spirit of Lydia Carpenter, a family servant of the Hale family whose apparition has been reported by a number of people, according to HauntedHouses.com.

Other ghostly manifestations the website mentions are phantom footsteps and chains clanking in the basement, even though there are none physically there to clank. One woman whose husband was a caretaker of the homestead for George Seymour believes the footsteps she heard stomping down the back stairs when she was the only one up were possibly those of John Hale or his wife and stepsister, Sarah, who died in the house in 1802 and 1803, respectively. The sound of someone pacing on the floors has also been reported. With a family so large, and with so many who died in that home, who it is that paces is anyone's guess.

When Nathan's brother Joseph was captured by the British while serving with the militia, he spent time chained in the cellar of a prison ship before being exchanged for a British soldier. That's why some believe the sound of chains clanking in the homestead's basement is the ghost of Joseph Hale.

George Seymour must have been delighted to include his own personal experience in his collection of legends and ghost stories of the Hale family. Shortly after he purchased the property, he brought a friend out to see it. According to HauntedHouses.com, his friend jumped from the buggy and ran up to the schoolroom to look in the window. The ghost of Deacon Richard Hale looked out of the window from inside the schoolroom to see who was coming at the very moment that Seymour's friend pressed his nose to the glass. I wonder who disappeared quicker—Deacon Hale, who stepped back into the room and instantly vanished, or Seymour's stunned friend, who stepped away from the window and made haste back to the buggy?

Things seem to have settled down at the old homestead. Staff members haven't seen or felt anything paranormal in years . . . at least, not on their watch. But the previously reported hauntings typically took place during the night or early-morning hours, when the staff is not on hand to experience them. Make of that what you will.

Homespun Farm

Kate and Ron Bauer purchased the 266-year-old Brewster House at 306 Preston Road in Griswold in 1996 and have lovingly turned it into an expanding two-guestroom bed-and-breakfast now called Homespun Farm. In December 2000, it was listed on the National Register of Historic Places, and rightfully so. The house was built in 1740 by Simon Brewster, the great-great-grandson of William Brewster, who came over on the *Mayflower*. It remained in the Brewster family until 1991, when the descendants decided they no longer wanted to run the large farm that once produced some of the country's best milk, as well as fruit in its orchards. The people who bought it from the Brewsters at auction never moved into the house or did anything to preserve the property. Nevertheless, the Bauers fell in love at first sight with the run-down house and quickly decided to become the second family name ever attached to the Colonial dwelling. Since that day, they've poured their heart and soul into the venture, and it shows from the moment you step onto their property.

Because of the Bauers' diligent efforts, hard work, and creative touches, Homespun Farm is truly a gem among Connecticut inns. The ghosts that oversee daily operations, occasionally offering subliminal advice, only add to its charm. Kate was the first to see Old Man Simon. She was pruning the blueberry patch when she saw a man to her left in her peripheral vision watching her and heard his telepathic advice: "No, no, no—not there." Luckily, Kate, who is a certified master gardener, wasn't offended by the input. But being a nonbeliever in ghosts at the time, she tried to discount her experience, until her husband told her of his own similar experience about a month later. The couple agreed that the apparition they'd both witnessed and "heard" in the garden was harmless. In fact, they call him a "watchful spirit" and feel quite comfortable with his presence.

The Bauers later described the man to a guest, and the woman showed them pictures of one of the original owners, named Simon Brewster. While Old Man Simon watches over the gardens and orchards, his wife seems to watch over the interior of the house. Kate said they've sometimes felt Mrs. Brewster's gentle presence inside, watching them. They hear her walking up the stairs in the night and feel that she's just making sure all's well when the lights go out.

Today Homespun Farm is a popular and award-winning bed-and-breakfast, hosting 350 visitors a year. As word of the inn's friendly ghosts spreads, more and more guests are now coming specifically to ghost hunt.

The John York House

The house built by John York, a North Stonington farmer and businessman, in 1741 was his private residence until the Revolutionary War, when opportunity knocked and he turned it into a tavern—a decision he likely lived to regret. After a bitter feud at the tavern left two soldiers dead, it wasn't long before it was turned back into a private residence. In 1997, it finally became an inn once again, called the John York House, and it's reported to be haunted, thanks to the unfortunate incidents that took place there during the Revolutionary War.

Two Continental Army soldiers who happened to be best friends were enjoying themselves at John York's in the Great West Room, which today is the library, when they came to the slow realization that they both had affections and intentions toward the same lovely young lady. The friendly banter turned confrontational and soon escalated into an all-out heated argument. Before anyone knew it, the buddies were involved in an ugly physical altercation that culminated with one man plunging a knife into the other, mortally wounding his comrade. The guilty party then fled into the night, without the woman he'd killed for or, sadly, his buddy. Alone and guilt-ridden, he committed suicide shortly thereafter. That's when the hauntings began.

Hauntings at the John York House have been documented since at least the early 1900s, but rumored ghost stories have been around since the 1700s. It began with mundane and mild phenomena, such as unexplained sounds, shadows seen out of the corner of the eye, and cold spots. Nothing too frightening, yet enough to make one recognize that something was amiss. Then in 1963, according to *Haunted Inns of New England,* a woman purchased the home, and in a misguided effort to find the source of the ghostly sounds, she held a séance or two.

The woman soon found that the benign, unexplainable sounds were nothing compared with the events that soon followed her first séance. Furniture was flipped over by unseen hands, a barometer repeatedly became a projectile, and the ominous sound of footsteps was heard frequently, rather than occasionally as had previously been the case. Locked doors were found opened, electrical objects turned themselves on and off, tobacco smoke was smelled, and loud bangs like cannon fire were heard.

The climax for that particular family was when their son awoke screaming one night, and his parents found him gagging, with red welts forming around his neck, as if someone were trying to strangle him right in front of them. They called in psychics, who sensed the presence of a Revolutionary War soldier consumed in guilt and in the throes of a temper tantrum. The psychics performed a ritual to send the departed souls on, and that seemed to work. Today the hauntings are few and far between. Still, when they do occur, they are unforgettable, such as when a minivan window exploded for no apparent reason as the friend of a more recent owner pulled up to the house, and the time that same owner heard someone calling to her from the bottom of the stairs but nobody was there. It appears, however, that for the most part, the ghosts are finally resting in peace.

Ledge Light

The Ledge Light is a remote, now fully automated lighthouse in New London Harbor that sits where Long Island Sound, the Thames River, and Fisher's Island Sound all come together. Built in 1909, the imposing brick building, which looks like a Georgian-style house floating on top of the water, has somehow withstood the harsh elements where many others have failed, including a steamship called *Atlantic* that slammed into Fisher's Island during a brutal November storm in 1846. Forty-two passengers and crewmembers were killed, including the priest and the captain. For more than a hundred years, the ship's sunken fog bell has been heard by many people, both ashore and at sea, reverberating across Long Island Sound, just as it did the night it guided the rescue boat to the battered wreckage as it rolled across the choppy sea. But this story is not about the phantom bell that tolls . . . or even the lost souls of the steamship *Atlantic*. It is about Ernie, the celebrated ghost of Ledge Light.

Since at least 1936, when lighthouse keeper John "Ernie" Randolph was said to have killed himself, someone has been haunting the Ledge Light. The events at the lighthouse give new meaning to the term "automated lighthouse." Many things have occurred there that would have required human effort, but nobody was present. The decks got washed, invisibly. While the lighthouse was still being manned, the televisions and foghorn turned themselves on and off, and doors—including that on the refrigerator—opened and closed, fully unassisted by human hands. Boats that had been securely tied up were often found drifting away. An old radio, when moved out of its usual spot, would be found repositioned in its original location the next day. An occasional decomposing-body smell was reported, as were apparitions seen only by women and children. One woman, according to *The Ghostly Register*, described the apparition that woke her one night as a tall, slim man with a beard, wearing a rain hat and raincoat. A lighthouse keeper of more recent times reported that he sometimes heard his name being called as he descended the ladder, when he was alone in the building. Obviously, this was a ghost who wanted attention and knew how to get it.

Why would Ernie haunt the place, if there was indeed a John "Ernie" Randolph? According to a combination of stories regarding Ernie from many different sources, he was keeper of the Ledge Light for only a few months in 1936, until he slashed his own throat and fell to the rocks surrounding the lighthouse. Ernie had married a young lady half his age, and the two enjoyed an extended honeymoon in their solitary confines, but the woman eventually grew to despise the place she found herself in and the man she found herself with. She longed for contact with the outside world. The loneliness of lighthouse living was simply not for her. Ernie was unsympathetic to his young bride's longings, and the two argued constantly. Ernie said some things he undoubtedly regretted, and his wife took the first opportunity she had to escape from the island. Details differ among sources as to whom she left with and where they ended up, but most say she ran off with a ferryboat captain making his way to New York. When Ernie realized that his harsh words and uncaring, unyielding ways had cost him his wife, he is said to have slit his own throat for speaking too much, before casting himself off the roof of the house. Nobody knows why he would take his life so hastily and then refuse to leave, but apparently this was the case, for the hauntings began shortly after his body was discovered.

After years of being manned by a number of lighthouse keepers, often someone off the street that could be persuaded to go into solitary confinement for a period of time, the lighthouse eventually was taken over by the Coast Guard in 1939. Many cadets and guardsmen started reporting strange happenings at Ledge Light. The very last entry in the log before the lighthouse became fully automated in 1987 says, "A rock of slow torture, hell on earth . . . it's Ernie's domain now." The only way to visit is by taking a summer tour of the lighthouse offered by Project Oceanology of Groton.

The Lighthouse Inn

New London's Lighthouse Inn Resort and Conference Center began as a Mediterranean-style country home for steel magnate Charles S. Guthrie. When he had the mansion overlooking Long Island Sound built in 1902, he asked noted Central Park designer Frederick Law Olmsted to coordinate the construction of the grounds. When the project was complete, Guthrie called his creation Meadow Court, for the wildflowers that blanketed the lawn of the mansion. The design of the mansion was nothing short of genius. Guthrie had it built in the shape of a half-circle to offer twenty-seven guest rooms a view of either the ocean or the gardens. *American Homes and Gardens* in 1912 said of the property, "There are few homes in America more attractively situated than the property of Mrs. Charles S. Guthrie."

Indeed, it was the envy of high society, and when it opened as the Lighthouse Inn in 1927, it was at once graced by the patronage of such Hollywood legends as Bette Davis and Joan Crawford. The inn was named after the nearby New London Harbor Light lighthouse, very haunted in its own right. The Lighthouse Inn was an enviable location to host a wedding and reception, with its lavishly flowered grounds, posh interior, and winding grand staircase for the bride to descend.

One particular bride, it is said, was so eager to make a grand entrance on her wedding day that she rehearsed the way she would carry herself gracefully down the staircase many times, until she had it as close to perfect as possible. She didn't want any mishaps. Tragically, on her wedding day in 1920, as she carefully descended the staircase to approach her waiting groom, she stumbled and fell, broke her neck, and died, never having made it into the waiting arms of her fiancé . . . never completing the procession she had practiced so many times. Many believe she still lingers in the stairway, following each bride down the steps to ensure that she doesn't stumble. Or perhaps she is still practicing her careful steps, day after day, for all of eternity, unaware that it's all for naught.

Sightings have been reported of a phantom bride reading in one of the guest rooms and roaming through some of the rooms, especially on the third floor. The inn is so famously haunted that The Atlantic Paranormal Society (TAPS) filmed an episode of *Ghost Hunters* there. During their investigation, one member of the crew felt someone touch him on the back, even though nobody was immediately behind him. The crew also recorded unexplained temperature drops, a phenomenon long associated with a ghostly presence. One employee told a visitor about something inexplicable she had experienced. She was in the basement alone when she heard a whooshing sound and saw a padlock on the gate of the liquor storage unit swinging rapidly back and forth, as if someone were in a hurry to get to the booze. Maybe it was the ill-fated bride, and you couldn't really blame her, after the ordeal she's been through!

Micah Rood's Curse

In Charles Skinner's *Myths and Legends of Our Own Land: Tales of Puritan Land* is a sordid tale about how Connecticut's Micah Rood apples got their name, and it's not as all-American as apple pie:

> "In Western Florida they will show roses to you that drop red dew, like blood, and have been doing so these many years, for they

sprang out of the graves of women and children who had been cruelly killed by Indians. But there is something queerer still about the Micah Rood—or 'Mike'—apples of Franklin, Connecticut, which are sweet, red of skin, snowy of pulp, and have a red spot, like a blood-drop, near the core; hence, they are sometimes known as bloody-hearts. Micah Rood was a farmer in Franklin in 1693. Though avaricious, he was somewhat lazy and was more prone to dream of wealth than to work for it. But people whispered that he did some hard and sharp work on the night after the peddler came to town—the slender man with a pack filled with jewelry and knickknacks—because on the morning after that visit, the peddler was found beneath an apple tree on Rood farm with his pack rifled and his skull split open.

"Suspicion pointed at Rood; and, while nothing was proved against him, he became gloomy, solitary, and morose, keeping his own counsels more faithfully than ever—though he never was disposed to take counsel of other people. If he had expected to profit by the crime, he was obviously disappointed, for he became poorer than ever, and his farm yielded less and less. To be sure, he did little work on it. When the apples ripened on the tree that had spread its branches above the peddler's body, the neighbors wagged their heads and whispered the more, for in the centre of each apple was a drop of the peddler's blood: a silent witness and judgment, they said, and the result of a curse that the dying man had invoked against his murderer. Micah Rood died soon after, without saying anything that his fellow villagers might be waiting to hear, but his tree is still alive and its strange fruit has been grafted on hundreds of orchards."

Skinner wasn't the only one to promulgate the legend. It became so famous that dictionaries and other resource books of the time included various descriptions of Micah Rood's apples. The *Dictionary of Phrase and Fable* described Micah Rood apples as follows: "Apples with a spot of red (like blood) in the heart. Micah Rood was a prosperous farmer at Franklin. In 1693, a peddler with jewelry called at his house and the next day was found murdered under an apple tree in Rood's orchard. The crime was never brought home to the farmer, but next autumn all the apples of the fatal tree bore inside a red blood-spot, called 'Micah Rood's Curse,' and the farmer died soon afterwards."

New London's Lost Treasure

The *Saints Joseph and Helena,* a Spanish galleon that was making its way from Havana, Cuba, to Cadiz, Spain, in 1753, went off course in stormy seas and slammed against a reef at New London, Connecticut, causing damage that required immediate repair. The freight was removed and put on shore to make room aboard for repair, and the collector of the port was in charge of watching the freight. But when it came time to set sail, a quarter of the cargo had disappeared mysteriously. The robbery gave New London a bad name in a very competitive shipping market. In fact, the governor lost the election because he didn't "make good the shortage."

Charles Skinner wrote of the lost precious cargo in *Myths and Legends of Our Own Land: As to Buried Treasure:*

It was reputed that some of the treasure was buried on the shore by the robbers. In 1827, a woman who was understood to have the power of seer-ship provided a vision to a couple of young blades, who had paid for it, to the effect that hidden beneath one of the grass-grown wharves was a box of dollars. By the aid of a crystal pebble, she received this valuable information, but the pebble was not clear enough to reveal the exact place of the box. She could see, however, that the dollars were packed edgewise.

"When New London was sound asleep, the young men stole out and, by lantern-light, began their work. They had dug to water-level when they reached an iron chest, and they stooped to lift it; but, to their amazement, the iron was too hot to handle! Now they heard deep growls, and a giant dog peered at them from the pit-mouth; red eyes flashed at them from the darkness; a wild-goose, with eyes of blazing green, hovered and screamed above them. Though the witch had promised them safety, nothing appeared to ward off the fantastic shapes that began to crowd about them. Too terrified to work any longer, they sprang out and made away; and, when taking courage from the sunshine they renewed the search the next day, the iron chest had vanished.

Somehow we knew how that one was going to end, didn't we?

Nightmare at Frog Pond

Practically every town or village has its claim to fame—a story or event so titillating that it goes down in local, if not national, history and is thereafter mentioned in every book or article ever written about the village. If it's really good, it gets incorporated into the village's seal, official logo, and letterhead. Mighty monuments are erected in its honor. Songs, and even operettas, are written memorializing the occasion or person . . . or frogs. Yes, frogs. The ruckus created by Windham's bullfrog population one fateful night in 1754 ensured that all future frogs of that village would forever be deified.

It was a cloudy, scorching night in July when the thousand or so residents of Windham were awakened by unidentifiable screams of agony or anger. Was it their worst fear—that the savages had come to rape and pillage their village at the start of the French and Indian War? Was it witches or devils flying overhead? Was it Doomsday? The hideous racket was so loud that it seemed as if it were directly above and surrounding them. Many undoubtedly snatched their Bibles from their nightstands and held them close to their hearts as they hid beneath their bedcovers. The women likely gathered up the young ones in their arms and embraced them tightly, while husbands and sons grimly set out well armed for what might be the bloody battle long rumored to be coming. The determined men fired their guns blindly into the night in the direction of the sound, for their enemy was imperceivable, until all of their ammunition was spent.

The peculiar screaming continued. The only thing that stifled the horrible clamor was time. By dawn, the sounds had finally faded away, and the villagers quickly set about searching for the source of the commotion they had been unable to identify in the dark. Thankfully, they determined that nobody had died, and there apparently had been no Indians in the area. So who were the culprits, for it certainly sounded like more than one, and what made them stop screaming?

According to the Windham Historical Society: "The light of day brought the scare to an end. What remained in the valley below Mullin Hill were thousands of frog corpses, lying all around on the banks of Frog Pond." Nobody ever determined what caused the bloodless frog massacre, though villagers at the time speculated that they had been diseased or suffered group panic at the realization that their water supply was drying up as a result of a drought. Perhaps they were poisoned or a strange atmospheric anomaly was responsible. Froggy heatstroke? Their bodies were all found lying belly-up. Whatever it was, it was certainly a strange phenomenon.

Charles M. Skinner, in *Myths and Legends of Our Own Land: Tales of Puritan Land,* explained it thus: "All night the greatest alarm prevailed. At early dawn, an armed party climbed the hill to the eastward, and seeing no sign of Indians or other invaders, returned to give comfort to their friends. . . . Next day, the reason of it all came out: a pond having been emptied by drought, the frogs that had lived there emigrated by common consent to a ditch nearer the town, and on arriving there had apparently fought for its possession, for many lay dead on the bank."

Skinner went on to say that one of the theories at the time of the frog uproar had a political spin to it, as an election was under way. "A contest for office was waging at that period between two lawyers, Colonel Dyer and Mr. Elderkin, and sundry of the people vowed that they had heard a challenging yell of 'Colonel Dyer! Colonel Dyer!' answered by a guttural defiance of 'Elderkin, too! Elderkin, too!' The night was still and the voices of the contestants sounded clearly into the village, the piping of the smaller being construed into 'Colonel Dyer,' and the grumble of the bull-frogs into 'Elderkin, too.' The 'frog scare' was a subject of pleasantry directed against Windham for years afterward."

More recently, David E. Philips described the incident in *Legendary Connecticut:* "Around the shore of the small mill pond and along the banks of the little stream that bubbled out of the pond to the south lay the belly-up bodies of hundreds, maybe even thousands, of bullfrogs!" He went on to say, in his delightful way: "On the night of the horrible outcry, something must have finally snapped in the frog community. . . . The result was a batrachian battle royal, complete with anguished croaks of the dying, and little green casualties beyond any accurate body count."

According to the Windham Historical Society, the pond that was the site of the unsolved mystery is located about a mile east of the old village (Windham Center) on Route 14, going toward Scotland. The pond is on the north side of the road, and a bronze plaque set in granite memorializes the spot where the famous frog massacre occurred.

Randall's Ordinary Landmark Inn

The Randalls were movers and shakers of both England and New England during the Colonial era. Matthew Randall was lord mayor of Bath, England, in 1629. His son John was a wealthy silk merchant in London, whose wife was the sister of Sir William Morton, founder of New London, Connecticut. John and his wife, Elizabeth Morton, purchased land in Stonington, Connecticut, in 1680, and five years later, their son John Randall II built the farmhouse that today is known as Randall's Ordinary Landmark Inn & Restaurant on Route 2 in North Stonington. Of course, if it's in this book, it has to be anything but ordinary.

The Randalls were not only lords, governors, commanding officers, and captains in the Continental Army, but also ardent abolitionists, among the first to set their slaves free. So it made sense that the home, which stayed in the Randall family until the late 1800s, had a trapdoor installed in the hearth room that led to a secret room where slaves were once hidden—a common element of ghost stories, it seems. Harvey Perry purchased and restored the homestead in 1926, but it wasn't opened as an inn until 1987. Today it is owned by the Mashantucket Pequot tribal nation, which works diligently to preserve the historic property and maintain the meticulous restoration Perry lovingly provided. There are fifteen guestrooms, twelve of which are located in the property's barn, built in 1819. On the second floor of the inn proper is an exquisite Colonial restaurant.

According to *Haunted Inns of New England,* guests have reported seeing a tall, slim older gentleman dressed in a uniform and carrying an early gun. He has a forlorn expression and has been seen with a child holding on to his leg. A psychic who investigated Room 12 said she felt he hid in the closet. He is believed to be responsible for the lights in the room flickering on and off and jiggling the latch on the attic door of that room. One guest heard what sounded like someone falling down the steps from the attic and landing against the door to that room, and a guest in the adjacent room heard the same sound at the same time.

The Inn's website says that staffers and guests alike believe they have seen or heard John Randall moving about the upper floor, and claims: "Eerily, everyone who has witnessed this ghost describes him the same way, a sad looking man with long hair. He is always seen wearing a uniform and carrying a blunderbuss, an old rifle with a muzzle that fans out like a tulip." Other than turning on and off lights and making noise in the hallway, their ghost is "essentially harmless." His favorite room to haunt is said to be Room 12. Other guests have had unexplained experiences in Rooms 6 and 11, such as feeling the sensation of someone sitting on the foot of the bed in Room 6, and then seeing a ghost get up and walk up the stairs and straight through the door without even opening it. So if ghosts and good food and authentic Colonial surroundings are your thing, Randall's Ordinary is a hard place to top.

Red Brook Inn

The Red Brook Inn bed-and-breakfast, just off the Gold Star Highway in Mystic, is also known as the Crary Homestead (circa 1770). Ruth Keyes purchased the historic Crary Homestead in 1980 and two years later opened it as a three-guest-room bed-and-breakfast that she called the Red Brook Inn.

Nancy Crary was born in the Crary House in 1820. Many believe that the gray-haired woman wearing a shawl who saved the lives of guests in the North Room on the second floor of the Crary House is the spirit of Nancy Crary. On both occasions, the lodgers forgot to open their fireplace flue after starting a fire—and on both occasions, the would-be victims fell asleep while the room filled with smoke and were awakened by the woman in the shawl. It's more likely that the heroic spirit is Nancy than another woman who died in the home years later. That one had a grudge to hold.

The story goes that many years ago, a previous owner of the Crary House fell in love with his wife's best friend. He begged forgiveness after his wife discovered the affair, and she conceded, but with one measly condition. She demanded his assurance that her ex-best friend never again set foot in their home. The husband kept his promise for twelve long years, but shortly after his wife died, he married her former best friend and moved out of his beloved Crary House and into his new bride's home across town.

Fast-forward many years. Ruth Keyes was now the owner of Crary House, and she received a phone call from the man's second wife asking if she could book the house to host his seventy-fifth birthday party, since he was so fond of his old home. Twice when the woman who was banned from the house visited to make arrangements for the party, a horrible stench, like rotting meat or a decaying corpse, followed her into each room. When she left, the smell dissipated. Ruth was perplexed, and a bit worried about guests' reactions to the odor at the upcoming party, until a friend offered as plausible an explanation as any. He told her that sometimes ghosts can emit foul smells if they are upset—and I'd hazard to say there's a pretty good chance the first wife was extremely upset that her admonition many years earlier had been disregarded. Sure enough, everything smelled like roses until the day of the party . . . when the banned woman arrived. Guests stifled revolted faces as their hostess made her way from room to room, with a trail of stench seeming to be right at her heels. As if that weren't enough of an insult to the party, when it came time to cut the carrot cake, it crumbled into hundreds of tiny pieces, leaving everyone empty-handed. This was a cake made at the finest bakery in town, and its implosion had to have broken some law of physics. I'd say the first Mrs. got even that day—and she's been quiet ever since. Now the only ghost left is the one who makes sure you sleep safe and sound, with your fire roaring and your flue open.

Vampires in Their Midst

Griswold is a lovely rural New England town. But much like Bela Lugosi's 1931 portrayal of Dracula, beneath the charm and appeal of its outward appearance lurks a dark and gruesome past. The proverbial skeletons in Griswold's closet found their way out in the fall of 1990, when a couple of youngsters playing on an eroding hill in a privately owned gravel and sand pit discovered two human skulls that landed practically at their feet.

The yearlong excavation and investigation that followed led to the discovery of twenty-nine individual skeletal remains, eventually determined to belong to the Walton family of Jewett City—a section of Griswold—who buried their members in a family plot there from about 1750 until the mid-1800s. That in itself wasn't particularly striking; however, the unusual manner in which three of the corpses were positioned warranted a thorough forensic examination and historic research to determine cause of death, if only for curiosity's sake. The findings determined that several members of the Walton family apparently had been thought to be vampires, for their bodies were disposed of using European vampire-vanquishing protocol of the 1700s. The undated and undocumented skeletal remains had the thigh bones positioned in a cross formation on top of the ribs and the skulls turned to face west, creating a skull-and-crossbones configuration. Such an arrangement was believed to release a soul from an eternity of vampirism. But why would anyone believe members of the Walton family—or any God-fearing nineteenth-century New England family—could possibly be vampires?

Vampire belief was alive and well in nineteenth-century New England . . . and so was tuberculosis, known then as consumption, a disease whose symptoms were often associated with vampires. In the 1800s, when the contagious disease was so prevalent, vaccines and antibiotics were not available. In those days, when one family member died of consumption, others often became ill within a couple years, suffering from the telltale wasting away of the body, as if the body were being slowly consumed, hence the term "consumption." Because vampires have long been accused of sucking the blood and life out of people, like the unforgiving disease seemed to do, consumption was often blamed on vampires rather than contagion.

Paleopathological evidence of the remains of the three individuals in the Walton cemetery whose skeletons were specifically arranged as if the family were dealing with vampires revealed signs of pulmonary tuberculosis, which likely led to their death. When the three came down with the dreaded disease one after the other, the rest of the family may have panicked and taken what they believed were the necessary actions to prevent any more stealing of life in their community by vampires. None of the other twenty-six bodies showed signs of infectious tuberculosis on medical analyses. So the remaining family members must have felt they had succeeded in vanquishing the vampires in their midst, further supporting the assumed validity of their misguided beliefs.

The Waltons weren't the only ones in the Jewett City–Griswold area who believed they were under attack by vampires. The Rays were also fighting their own battle with familial vampires in the mid-1800s, about the same time the Waltons suffered their ordeal.

Horace (or by some accounts, Henry) Ray had five children. In 1845, twenty-five-year-old son Lemuel died, presumably of consumption. Four years later, the father was stricken with the same illness and laid to rest beside his son in the Jewett City Cemetery. Two years later, in 1851, twenty-six-year-old Elisha succumbed to the same fate as his father and brother. Finally, when the oldest son, Henry, showed signs of consumption just three years later, a group of family members and close friends decided to take matters into their own hands and put an end to the madness. Dudley Wright, in *The Book of Vampires,* said the plan of the panicked family was "to exhume the bodies of the two brothers and burn them, because the dead were supposed to feed upon the living; and so long as the dead body in the grave remained un-decomposed, either wholly or in part, the surviving members of the family must continue to furnish substance on which the dead body could feed. Acting under the influence of this strange superstition, the family and friends of the deceased proceeded to the burial ground on June 8, 1854, dug up the bodies of the deceased brothers, and burned them on the spot."

According to a government document titled "Bioarcheological and Biocultural Evidence for the New England Vampire Folk Belief," many eighteenth-century Europeans and New Englanders believed certain traits would be present on an exhumed body of an actual vampire. A "bloated chest, long fingernails, and blood draining from the mouth" were sure signs that the vampire was draining life from the living. Today these are known to be normal characteristics of postmortem decomposition, but one or two centuries ago, if such traits were present, either the blood-filled heart of the cadaver or the entire body would often be removed from the grave and burned to ensure death to the vampire.

Of the twelve historic accounts of vampires in eighteenth- and nineteenth-century New England—specifically, in Connecticut, Vermont, Rhode Island, and Massachusetts—all have been determined to have been cases of consumption.

Bibliography

Books and Articles

Bender, Albert K. *Flying Saucers and the Three Men*. Clarksburg, WV: Saucerian Books, 1963.

Brewer, Ebeneezer Cobham. *Dictionary of Phrase and Fable*. Philadelphia: Henry Altemus Company, 1894.

Clark, Jerome. *Unexplained!* Canton, MI: Visible Ink Press, 1999.

Eno, Paul F. *Faces at the Window*. Woonsockett, RI: New River Press, 1998.

Frost, Scott. *The Annual Register of World Events, 1758–1963*. London: Longman, 1964.

Godbeer, Richard. *Escaping Salem: The Other Witch Hunt of 1692*. New York: Oxford University Press, 2004.

Jasper, Mark. *Haunted Inns of New England*. Yarmouth Port, MA: On Cape Publications, 2000.

Myers, Arthur. *The Ghostly Register*. New York: McGraw-Hill/Contemporary Books, 1986.

Philips, David E. *Legendary Connecticut: Traditional Tales from the Nutmeg State*. Willimantic, CT: Curbstone Press, 1992.

Pitkin, David. *Ghosts of the Northeast*. New York: Aurora Publications, 2002.

Pynchon, W. H. C. "The Black Dog." *Connecticut Quarterly*, 1898.

Schlosser, S. E. *Spooky New England: Tales of Hauntings, Strange Happenings, and Other Local Lore*. Guilford, CT: Globe Pequot, 2003.

Shepard, Odell. *The Harvest of a Quiet Eye*. Boston: Houghton Mifflin Company, 1927.

Skinner, Charles M. *Myths and Legends of Our Own Land: As to Buried Treasure and Storied Waters, Cliffs, and Mountains*. Philadelphia: J. B. Lippincott, 1896.

———. *Myths and Legends of Our Own Land: Tales of Puritan Land.* Philadelphia: J. B. Lippincott, 1896.

Warren, Ed, and Lorraine Warren. *Graveyard.* New York: St. Martin's Paperbacks, Reprint edition.

Wright, Dudley. *The Book of Vampires.* New York: Causeway Books, 1973.

Online Sources
(in order by story)

"Connecticut Tourism Regions," *Connecticut Bound Vacation.* Retrieved 27 April 2005. www.ctbound.org.

"Connecticut," *888-CTvisit / CTvisit.com.* Retrieved 14 September 2005. www.tourism.state.ct.us.

"Spirited Happenings at Connecticut Haunted Restaurant." *Far Shores Paranormal Pages.* Retrieved 27 April 2005. www.100megsfree4.com/farshores/phaunt2.htm.

"Happenings at Carousel Gardens." *Carousel Gardens: Happenings.* Retrieved 4 May 2005. www.carouselgardens.com/happenings.html.

Belanger, Jeff. "Dudleytown—A New England Ghost Town." *Legends of the Supernatural.* Retrieved 20 September 2005. www.ghostvillage.com/legends/dudleytown.htm.

"2000 Ghost Encounters at Ghostvillage.com." *GhostVillage.com.* Retrieved 20 September 2005. www.ghostvillage.com/encounters/2000index.htm.

"Cursed Dudleytown Ghost Village." *Roadside America.* Retrieved 14 September 2005. www.roadsideamerica.com.

Georgantas, Will. "Thrill-Seekers Go Home. The Dudleytown Curse, Cornwall, Conn." *Hartford Advocate: Things Get Curiouser & Curiouser . . .* Retrieved 5 May 2005. www.hartfordadvocate.com.

Taylor, Troy. "Dudleytown—An Enduring Enigma of the Connecticut Mountains." *Prairie Ghosts.* Retrieved 27 April 2005. www.prairieghosts.com/dudleytown.html.

"MUFON CT Cases." *Mutual UFO Network of CT—MUFON CT Cases.* Retrieved 13 May 2005. www.temporaldoorway.com/mufonct/report/mufon.htm.

"Connecticut Sightings of the Hudson Valley 'Boomerang' as Investigated by Mark Packo." *Mutual UFO Network of CT.* Retrieved 14 September 2005. http://temporaldoorway.com/mufonct/report/packoreportonhudsonvalley.htm.

Imbrogno, Philip J. "The Hudson Valley Sightings." *UFO Area.* Retrieved 20 September 2005. www.ufoarea.com/events_hudson_valley.html.

"Guntown Cemetery." *Ghostwatcherz.com.* Retrieved 9 December 2005. http://ghostwatcherz.com/guntown.php.

Bibliography

"Guntown Cemetery, Naugatuck." *Haunted Connecticut at All about Ghosts—Your Paranormal Portal.* Retrieved 27 April 2005. http://dawghouse.topcities.com/connecticut.html.

"Green Lady Cemetery." *Haunted Connecticut at All about Ghosts—Your Paranormal Portal.* Retrieved 27 April 2005. http://dawghouse.topcities.com/connecticut.html.

"Naugatuck—Guntown Cemetery." *Shadowlands Haunted Places Index—Connecticut.* Retrieved 2 May 2005. http://theshadowlands.net/places/connecticut.htm.

"Mount Dread. Holy Land USA, Waterbury, Conn." *Hartford Advocate: Things Get Curiouser & Curiouser . . .* Retrieved 5 May 2005. www.hartfordadvocate.com.

"Waterbury—Holy Land." *Shadowlands Haunted Places Index—Connecticut.* Retrieved 2 May 2005. http://theshadowlands.net/places/connecticut.htm.

Belanger, Jeff. "The Leatherman: Connecticut's Wandering Hobo." *Legends of the Supernatural.* Retrieved 27 April 2005. www.ghostvillage.com/legends/leatherman.htm.

Gengo, Lorraine. "He Had a Passion for Fashion." *Hartford Advocate: Things Get Curiouser & Curiouser . . .* Retrieved 5 May 2005. www.hartfordadvocate.com.

"About Lake Lillinonah." *Friends of the Lake.* Retrieved 16 November 2005. www.friendsofthelake.org/about_lake_lillinonah/.

Hamilton, Bobby. "From the Files of (GCBRO)." *Connecticut Litchfield County Bigfoot Reports.* Retrieved 2 May 2005. www.gcbro.com/CNlitch001.htm.

"From the Files of (GCBRO)." *Bigfoot Sightings.* Retrieved 2 May 2005. www.gcbro.com/CNlitch002.htm.

Brundage, Brita, and James Morgan. "Step Away from the Throne" and ". . . What Happens When You Don't." *Hartford Advocate: Things Get Curiouser & Curiouser . . .* Retrieved 5 May 2005. www.hartfordadvocate.com.

"Middlebury—Little People's Village." *Shadowlands Haunted Places Index—Connecticut.* Retrieved 2 May 2005. http://theshadowlands.net/places/connecticut.htm.

"Crazy Clouds and Fog." *When Nature Goes Nuts.* Retrieved 2 May 2005. http://paranormal.about.com/cs/earthanomalies/a/aa092203.htm.

Sheridan, Robert L. "1758." *Astronomical & Atmospheric Oddities.* Retrieved 2 May 2005. www.authorsden.com.

Heidorn, Keith C. "Weather Almanac for May 2004—New England's Dark Day." *The Weather Doctor Almanac 2004.* Retrieved 2 December 2005. www.islandnet.com/ ~ see/weather/almanac/arc2004/alm04may.htm.

"Portrait of a Family: Stamford through the Legacy of the Davenports—
Abraham Davenport & the Dark Day." *Stamford Historical Society.*
Retrieved 2 December 2005.
www.stamfordhistory.org/dav_whittier.htm.

"Dark Day." *Davenport Exhibit—Abraham Davenport.* Retrieved
2 December 2005. www.stamfordhistory.org/dav_ddpoem2.htm.

"Opening Revelation's Seven Seals." *These Last Days.* Retrieved
2 December 2005. www.champs-of-truth.com/lessons/booklet_A.htm.

"Chasing Away the Ghosts of Fairfield Hills' Reputation." *Ghost Hounds.*
Retrieved 10 November 2005. www.ghosthounds.com/modules
.php?name + News&file = article&sid = 142.

"We All Go a Little Mad Sometimes." *Fairfield County Weekly:
Things Get Curiouser & Curiouser . . .* Retrieved 10 November 2005.
www.westchesterweekly.com.

"Fairfield Hills." (forum) *The Smoking Gun Research Agency—SGRA.*
Retrieved 10 November 2005. www.sgra-media.com/modules
.php?name = Forums&file = viewtopic&t = 420&view = next.

"What Is Your State's Most Haunted "Famed" Place . . ." (forum) *TAPS.*
Retrieved 10 November 2005.
www.the-atlantic-paranormal-society.com/forums/index.php.

"Fairfield—Fairfield Hills Mental Institution." *Shadowlands Haunted
Places Index—Connecticut.* Retrieved 2 May 2005.
http://theshadowlands.net/places/connecticut.htm.

Driscoll, Eugene. "Warning: Stay Away from Fairfield Hills." *The News
Times.* Retrieved 10 November 2005. www.newstimes180.com.

Monroe Historical Society. "Hanna Cranna, the Witch of Old Monroe."
Old Homes of Monroe. Retrieved 16 November 2005.
www.monroehistoricsociety.org/hannacranna.html.

Cerullo, Michael. "Hannah Cranna." *Tangled Forest.* Retrieved
16 November 2005. www.tangledforest.com/tangledf/hannax.html.

Cerullo, Michael. "Phelps Mansion, aka the Stratford Knockings."
Tangled Forest. Retrieved 16 November 2005.
www.tangledforest.com/tangledf/phelpsx.html.

Taylor, Troy. "The Enigma of American Poltergeists—The Stratford
Poltergeist." *Prairie Ghosts.* Retrieved 16 November 2005.
www.prairieghosts.com/stratford.html.

"Phelps Mansion—Haunted Houses.com." *HauntedHouses.com.* Retrieved
16 November 2005. www.hauntedhouses.com/states/ct/house3.htm.

"The Phelps Mansion." *The Smoking Gun Research Agency—SGRA—The
Phelps Mansion.* Retrieved 16 November 2005. www.sgra-media.com/.

Kent, Donna. "Shakespeare Theatre." *Cosmic Society.* Retrieved 15
November 2005. www.cosmicsociety.com/shakespeare_theatre.htm.

Bibliography

"Department of Community/Economic Development November 2005." *Town of Stratford.* Retrieved 16 November 2005. www.townofstratford.com/businessnewswebnov2005.htm.

Best, Jonathon. "The Vision of Shakespeare." *BEST for Stratford.* Retrieved 16 November 2005. www.bestforstratford.com/SHAKESSPEECH.html.

Marcus, Ronald. "Elizabeth Clawson . . . Thou Deseruest to Dye." *The Trial of Elizabeth Clawson.* Retrieved 26 October 2005. http://rootsweb.com/ ~ ctfairfi/stamford/witch_trial1.htm.

Adams, Gretchen. "Hunting Witches . . . Responsibly." *Common-Place.* Retrieved 26 October 2005. www.common-place.org/vol-05/no-04/reviews/adams.shtml.

Schachter, Steven C., M.D. "Simple Partial Seizures." *Epilepsy.* Retrieved 6 December 2005. www.epilepsy.com/epilepsy/seizure_simplepartial.html.

Kent, Donna. "Union Cemetery & the White Lady." *Cosmic Society of Paranormal Investigation.* Retrieved 5 December 2005. www.cosmicsociety.com/unionc.htm.

Belanger, Jeff. "50 Years of Ghost Hunting and Research with the Warrens—Local Hauntings." *Ghost Village.* Retrieved 16 November 2005. www.ghostvillage.com/legends/warrens.htm.

Cerullo, Michael. "The White Lady." *Tangled Forest.* Retrieved 5 December 2005. www.tangledforest.com/tangledf/whiteladyx.html.

"Union Cemetery." *Ghosts of Connecticut.* Retrieved 16 November 2005. www.mysticalblaze.com/GhostsConnecticut.htm.

Landino, Dave. "Union Cemetery." *Real Ghosts—Union Cemetery.* Retrieved 16 November 2005. http://members.tripod.com/ ~ GSOLTESZ/union.htm.

"Daniel Benton Homestead, Tollan, CT." *The Cold Spot.* Retrieved 27 September 2005. www.theflagship.net/coldspot/docs/hauntedhistory-newengland.html.

"Tolland—the Benton Homestead." *Shadowlands Haunted Places Index—Connecticut.* Retrieved 2 May 2005. http://theshadowlands.net/places/connecticut.htm.

Philips, David E. "The Black Dog of West Peak." *Legendary Connecticut.* Retrieved 28 September 2005. www.curbstone.org/index.cfm?webpage = 107.

Russell, David. "Phantom Hounds." *Paranormal Phenomena.* Retrieved 28 September 2005. http://maxpages.com/mapit/PHANTOM_HOUNDS.

Schlosser, S. E. "The Black Dog of Hanging Hills." *American Folklore.* Retrieved 27 September 2005. www.americanfolklore.net/folktales/ct2.html.

Cerullo, Michael. "Black Dog of Hanging Hills." *Tangled Forest.* Retrieved 28 September 2005. www.tangledforest.com/tangledf/hanginghillx.html.

"A Legend." *City of Meriden.* Retrieved 28 September 2005. www.cityofmeriden.org.

Simonds, Hon. William E. "Canton, CT." *Rays Place.* Retrieved 16 November 2005. http://history.rays-place.com/ct/canton-ct.htm.

"Hopbox." *Letterboxing.org.* Retrieved 15 November 2005. www.letterboxing.org/BoxView.asp?boxnum = 8169&boxname = Hopbox.

"History." *CT DEP: Devil's Hopyard State Park.* Retrieved 15 November 2005. http://dep.state.ct.us/stateparks/parks/devilshopyard.htm.

"Devil's Hopyard State Park." *Acorn Bed & Breakfast.* Retrieved 15 November 2005. www.acornbedandbreakfast.com/devilshopyard.html.

"Gay City." *Gay City—Ghost Town.* Retrieved 1 December 2005. www.ghosttowns.com/states/ct/gaycity.html.

Helfferich, Carla. "Things That Go Boom in the Night, Article #896." *Alaska Science Forum.* Retrieved 15 November 2005. www.gi.alaska.edu/ScienceForum/ASF8/896.html.

DePold, Hans. "Ghosts of Bolton Past and Present." *Bolton News.* Retrieved 1 December 2005. www.boltonnews.org/zghosts.html.

———. "The Quarryville Boom Town." *Bolton Community News.* Retrieved 28 November 2005. www.boltonnews.org/zquarryville.html.

"Bolton (Connecticut) Historic Roads." *Bolton News.* Retrieved 12 January 2005. www.boltonnews.org/zboltonroads.html.

"Hartford—Old State House." *Shadowlands Haunted Places Index— Connecticut.* Retrieved 2 May 2005. http://theshadowlands.net/places/connecticut.htm.

"Old State House History." *Old State House.* Retrieved 15 November 2005. www.ctosh.org/history_vintphotos/osh_history.htm.

"Museum of Natural and Other Curiosities." *Old State House.* Retrieved 15 November 2005. www.ctosh.org/visit_the_osh/stewards_museum.htm.

"The 'Old' State House." *State of Connecticut Sites, Seals and Symbols.* Retrieved 21 November 2005. http://vvv.state.ct.us/emblems/sthouse.hTM.

"Exploration and Settlement of Connecticut." *U-S-history.com.* Retrieved 21 November 2005. www.u-s-history.com/pages/h543.html.

"Ghost Story—Abigail Pettibone." *Pettibone Tavern.* Retrieved 7 March 2005. http://pettibonetavern.com/abigail.html.

Pelkey, Karen. "Re-opened Tavern Features a Lot of History and a Hint of Mystery." *Imprint Newspapers.* Retrieved 15 November 2005. www.zwire.com/site/news.cfm?newsid = 7282866&BRD + 1666&PAG + 461&dept_id = 14030&rfi = 6.

"Businesses . . . Full of the Unexplained!" *Lucidct.com— On the Cover: Spirits of the Season.* Retrieved 15 November 2005. www.lucidct.com/cover/spooky3.html.

Trainor, Joseph. "Airplane Vanishes over Long Island Sound." *UFO Roundup, Vol. 2, No. 3.* Retrieved 15 November 2005. www.virtuallystrange.net/ufo/updates/1997/jan/m21-001.shtml.

"Phantom Plane Crashes." *Paranormal Phenomena.* Retrieved 15 November 2005. http://paranormal.about.com/library/weekly/aa062899.htm?iam + metaresults&terms = plane + crashes.

Klemsa, Marty. "Phantom Plane Crash and Green Fireballs." *Marty Klemsa's Official Website.* Retrieved 15 November 2005. www.erestor.net/show.cgi?x-files/twa800/twa-800.

"Near Landing at Old Saybrook, 12/15–16/57, Mary Starr." *Mutual UFO Network of CT.* Retrieved 28 September 2005. www.temporaldoorway.com/mufonct/report/571215.htm.

"UFOs in History—1957, Part 2." *The Bible UFO Connection.* Retrieved 28 September 2005. www.bibleufo.com/ufos921.htm.

"Close, but Not Close Enough, Encounters." *The Best of Hartford 2001.* Retrieved 28 September 2005. http://old.hartfordadvocate.com.

Wallace, Chevon. "Albert Bender and the M.I.B. Mystery." *Central High School—Albert Bender.* Retrieved 16 November 2005. http://bridgeport.ct.schoolwebpages.com/education/components/ scrapbook/default.php%3Fsectiondetailid + 25228.

Connors, Wendy A. "Peeking into the Old Saucer Bulletins of Days Slipped By." *Destination: Space UFO Template.* Retrieved 16 November 2005. www.destinationspace.net/ufo/connors/refugee.asp.

"Men in Black." *Metareligion.* Retrieved 16 November 2005. www.meta-religion.com/Paranormale/UFO/men_in_black.htm.

"Strange & Unexplained—Men in Black." *Sky Gaze.* Retrieved 6 December 2005. www.skygaze.com/content/strange/MenInBlack.shtml.

"Men in Black Facts." *Totse.* Retrieved 6 December 2005. www.totse.com/en/fringe/men_in_black/mibfacts.html.

"Men in Black, Part Two. Albert Bender and the Three Men in Black." *Think About-It.* Retrieved 6 December 2005. http://www.think-aboutit .com/ufo/albert_bender_and_the_three_men_.htm.

"Close Encounters with Mysterious 'Men in Black,' Part 1." *UFO Evidence.* Retrieved 5 December 2005. www.ufoevidence.org/documents/doc1695.htm.

Murphy, Linda. "A Review of MIBS (Men in Black): A History."
UFO Casebook. Retrieved 5 December 2005.
http://ufocasebook.com/meninblack.html.

Ellis, Parker. "Men in Black (MIBS)." *Alien Informants.* Retrieved
5 December 2005. www.informantnews.net/mib/mibs.html.

"A Rich History . . . " Milford, CT. Retrieved 2 May 2005.
http:www.milfordct.com/Page%204.pdf.

"Milford—Charles Island." *Shadowlands Haunted Places Index—
Connecticut.* Retrieved 2 May 2005.
http://theshadowlands.net/places/connecticut.htm.

"Iroquois Gas Transmission System Application for a Certificate of
Environmental Compatibility and Public Need. March 25, 2002."
Retrieved 21 November 2005. www.ogc.doc.gov/czma.nsf/
CCC16AC19FC95CA485256E13007330C9/$File/ccc16.pdf?.

"The Dark Spectre on Charles Island." *Trespassing Time.
Ghost Stories from the Prairie.* Retrieved 21 November 2005.
http://www.ghostvillage.com/encounters/2003/12122003.shtml.

"DEP Issues Emergency Closure of Charles and Duck Islands to Protect
Wildlife." *Connecticut Department of Environmental Protection.*
Retrieved 21 November 2005.
http://dep.state.ct.us/whatshap/press/2005/mf063005.htm.

"Silver Sands State Park." *Connecticut Department of Environmental
Protection.* Retrieved 21 November 2005.
http://dep.state.ct.us/stateparks/parks/silversands.htm.

Schurman, Kathleen. "This Island's for the Birds." *Milford Mirror*
(April 11, 2001). Retrieved 22 November 2005.
www.zwire.com/news/newsstory.cfm?newsid = 1661919&BRD =
1347&PAG = 461.

"Fort Nathan Hale." *GhostPlaces.com—CT Hauntings.* Retrieved
16 November 2005. http://e-clipse.com/gp/connecticut.htm.

"Fort Nathan Hale History." *Fort Nathan Hale—Black Rock Fort.*
Retrieved 16 November 2005. www.fort-nathan-hale.org./history.html.

"Welcome to Fort Nathan Hale." *Fort Nathan Hale—Black Rock Fort.*
Retrieved 16 November 2005. www.fort-nathan-hale.org./index.html.

"Connecticut—Black Rock Fort (2)." *American Forts East.*
Retrieved 28 November 2005. www.geocities.com/naforts/ct.html.

"Fort History." *Fort Nathan Hale Engineers.* Retrieved 29 November 2005.
http://fortmaps.tripod.com/.

"Annual Re-enactment of the July 1779 British Invasion of New Haven."
Second Company Governor's Foot Guard. Retrieved 28 November 2005.
www.footguard.org/hale.html.

"Haunted Places by State." *Winter Steel.* Retrieved 28 November 2005.
www.wintersteel.com/Haunted_Placesp2.html.

Bibliography

"New Haven, Connecticut—Midnight Mary Grave."
RoadsideAmerica.com. Retrieved 7 November 2005.
http://roadsideamerica.com/.

Stephenson, Carolyn F. "Connecticut Folklore: Fact or Fiction."
Yale-New Haven Teachers Institute. Retrieved 7 November 2005.
www.yale.edu/ynhti/curriculum/units/1987/4/87.04.05.x.html.

"Midnight Mary—Saturday, July 23, 2005." *The Daily Drink.*
Retrieved 21 November 2005.
http://dailyabuse.typepad.com/the_daily_drink/just_strange/.

"New Haven—The Old Union Trust Building." *Shadowlands Haunted
Places Index—Connecticut.* Retrieved 2 May 2005.
http://theshadowlands.net/places/connecticut.htm.

Joseph. "The Union Trust Haunting Photos." *The Haunted Skyscraper.*
Retrieved 7 November 2005.
www.geocities.com/epacel/The_Haunted_Skyscraper.html.html.

"The Most Mysterious House Ever Built." *The Most Mysterious House
Ever Built.* Retrieved 2 May 2005.
http://paranormal.about.com/library/weekly/aa052200a.htm.

"New Haven's Ronan-Edgehill Neighborhood." *New History.*
Retrieved 4 May 2005. www.sachem.org/newhistory.html.

Nickell, Joe. "Winchester Mystery House: Fact vs. Fancy.
(Investigative Files)." *Skeptical Inquirer.* September 9, 2002.
Retrieved 2 December 2005. www.highbeam.com/library/docfree.asp
?DOCID = 1G1:91236222&ctrlInfo = Round18%3AMode18c%3ADocG
%3AResult&ao.

Taylor, Troy. "The Winchester Mystery House: The History of One of
America's Most Haunted Houses." *Ghosts of the Prairie.* Retrieved
2 December 2005. www.prairieghosts.com/winchester.html.

Newitz, Annalee. "The Winchester Mystery House and Other Ghost
Stories of Industry in Silicon Valley." *Annalee Newitz—Recent
Presentation Papers.* Retrieved 5 December 2005.
www.techsploitation.com/socrates/Winchester_Silicon.html.

May, Antoinette. "The Winchester Mystery Mansion."
Ghosts of the World—Haunted Hamilton. Retrieved 3 December 2005.
www.hauntedhamilton.com/gotw_winchester.html.

"Marasmus." *Homeopathy for Everyone.* Retrieved 5 December 2005.
www.hpathy.com/diseases/marasmus.asp.

Mark, John T. "Sarah Winchester and Her Mystery House."
About Famous People. Retrieved 2 December 2005.
www.aboutfamouspeople.com/article1231.html.

"Town of Wallingford—Points of Interest." *Town of Wallingford.*
Retrieved 16 November 2005. www.town.wallingford.ct.us/
Page.cfm?name = Points%20of%20Interest.

Taylor, Troy. "The Man Who Could Fly?" *Prairie Ghosts.*
Retrieved 26 October 2005. www.prairieghosts.com/ddhome.html.

Lewis, David. "Is Anti-Gravity in Your Future?" *Atlantis Rising Magazine.*
Retrieved 26 October 2005.
www.atlantisrising.com/issue1/ar1antigrav.html.

"The Incredible Powers of D. D. Home."
The Incredible Powers of D. D. Home. Retrieved 2 May 2005.
http://paranormal.about.com/library/weekly/aa022403a.htm.

Cerullo, Michael. "Village of Voices, Bara-Hack." *Tangled Forest.* Retrieved
20 October 2005. www.tangledforest.com/tangledf/barahackx.html.

"Bara Hack." *Connecticut Paranormal Research Society.* Retrieved
20 October 2005. www.cprs.info/hauntedhouses/bara_hack.htm.

Abbott, Stephen. "The Bara Hack Investigation."
The Bara-Hack Investigation Web Site. Retrieved 20 October 2005.
www.sacomm.com/barahack.htm.

"Bara-Hack." *Bara-Hack—Ghost Town.* Retrieved 20 October 2005.
www.ghosttowns.com/states/ct/bara-hack.html.

"Captain Grant's, 1754—A National Historic Inn." *Captain Grant's, 1754.*
Retrieved 10 November 2005. www.captaingrants.com/.

"Captain Grant's, 1754." *New England Bed and Breakfast Inn Connecticut.*
Retrieved 10 November 2005.
www.virtualcities.com/ons/ct/z/ctz9701.htm.

Adamian, John. "The Stones of Groton." *Hartford Advocate.*
Retrieved 1 November 2005.
www.hartfordadvocate.com/gbase/Guides/content?oid = oid:7738.

"The Gungywamp Society." *The Gungywamp Society.* Retrieved
20 October 2005. www.gungywamp.com/index.html.

Angel, Paul Tudor. "Mystery Hill—America's Stonehenge."
Megaliths of New England. Retrieved 27 April 2005.
www.crystalinks.com/mysteryhill.html.

Timpanelli, N. L. "Connecticut." *Connecticut: Mysterious New England.*
Retrieved 20 October 2005. http://lithic.50g.com/conn.htm.

"The Hale Homestead—Hauntedhouses.com." *HauntedHouses.com.*
Retrieved 26 October 2005.
www.hauntedhouses.com/states/ct/house2.htm.

"The Homestead." *Nathan Hale Homestead.* Retrieved 26 October 2005.
http://ursamajor.hartnet.org/als/nathanhale/homestead.htm.

"Coventry—South Street—Hale Homestead." *Shadowlands
Haunted Places Index—Connecticut.* Retrieved 2 May 2005.
http://theshadowlands.net/places/connecticut.htm.

"Frequently Asked Questions." *Nathan Hale.* Retrieved 26 October 2005.
http://ursamajor.hartnet.org/als/nathanhale/faq.htm.

Bibliography

Pope, Janet. "A Tale of Two Lodgings." *The Celebrity Café.com*. Retrieved 26 October 2005. http://thecelebritycafe.com/travel/homespun_farms_2004_03-pl.html.

"Homespun Farm's 'Featured in' Page." *Homespun Farm—Articles on the Farm*. Retrieved 26 October 2005. www.homespunfarm.com/articles.html.

"Welcome to Homespun Farm B&B." *Homespun Farm*. Retrieved 18 November 2005. www.homespunfarm.com/.

Grote, David, and Leea Grote. "The John York House." *The John York House*. Retrieved 20 October 2005. http://members.tripod.com/jayboy74/story10.html.

"Groton—LedgeLight (Lighthouse)." *Shadowlands Haunted Places Index—Connecticut*. Retrieved 2 May 2005. http://theshadowlands.net/places/connecticut.htm.

"New London Ledge Lighthouse." *Haunted Lighthouses*. Retrieved 2 May 2005. http://paranormal.about.com/library/weekly/aa032601a.htm.

Forum. "The Lighthouse Inn—The White Lady." *The Atlantic Paranormal Society*. Retrieved 26 October 2005. www.the-atlantic-paranormal-society.com/forums/index.php.

"The Lighthouse Inn, Resort and Conference Center." *Historic Hotels of America*. Retrieved 18 November 2005. www.historichotels.org.

"The Battle of the Frogs." *Windham Historical Society*. Retrieved 19 October 2005. www.windhamhistory.org/frogs.shtml.

"Meet John Randall." *Randall's Ordinary*. Retrieved 14 September 2005. www.randallsordinary.com/history_john_randall.asp.

Cerullo, Michael. "Red Brook Inn." *Tangled Forest*. Retrieved 26 October 2005. www.tangledforest.com/tangledf/redbrookx.html.

Sledzik, Paul, and Nicholas Bellantoni. "Bioarcheological and Biocultural Evidence for the New England Vampire Folk Belief—from the *American Journal of Physical Anthropology* No. 94." *Evidence for New England Vampire Belief*. Retrieved 3 May 2005. http://users.net1plus.com/vyrdolak/NEfolkbelief.htm.

"Town of Griswold." *Connecticut's Mystic & More!* Retrieved 20 October 2005. www.mysticmore.com/sitemap/860_376_7061.html.

Acknowledgments

I'D LIKE TO THANK KYLE WEAVER, MY FAITHFUL EDITOR AT STACKPOLE Books, and his lovely assistant, associate editor Amy Cooper, and the rest of the staff at Stackpole. Much appreciation to artist Heather Adel for the atmospheric artwork that graces the covers and pages of this book, as well as *Haunted Massachusetts, Haunted New York,* and others in this series not written by me.

Many thanks to the people who gave me the nod to include various stories in this book or otherwise assisted me along the way, some of whom include: Joseph of "The Haunted Skyscraper" website, Maureen Clark and Karen Walkup of The Lighthouse Inn, Ron and Kate Bauer of Homespun Farm, Ted and Carol Matsumoto of Captain Grant's, 1754, and Ruth Keys of the Red Brook Inn.

I thank my four daughters, Michelle, Jamie, Katie, and Nicole. Through their eyes, I discover which stories hold the most appeal, especially to the younger crowd. We're talking five years old, with my little mini-me sitting on my lap asking me to tell her more! As always, I have to acknowledge my parents, Tom and Jean Dishaw; my brother, Tom; and my sisters, Cindy Barry and Chris Walker. Their support knows no bounds, and God knows I've tested that theory time and again. Special thanks to Leland Farnsworth for being there through thick and thin—especially thick—and for keeping me sane when it was all a blur. Mostly, I thank God for all of the above.

About the Author

CHERI REVAI IS THE AUTHOR OF THE BEST-SELLING THREE-BOOK SERIES *Haunted Northern New York,* as well as *Haunted Massachusetts: Ghosts & Strange Phenomena of the Bay State* and *Haunted New York: Ghosts & Strange Phenomena of the Empire State.* She is a North Country native who resides in northern New York with her family. A mother of four, she is also a secretary and an author who enjoys traveling, research, and history.